W9-ABT-612

DATE			

SEP   1996

BAKER & TAYLOR

Morrissey
Landscapes of the Mind

Morrissey
Landscapes of the Mind

Carroll & Graf Publishers, Inc.
New York

Published by arrangement with Robson Books, London.

First edition June 1995

Carroll & Graf Publishers, Inc.
260 Fifth Avenue
New York, NY 10001

ISBN: 0-7867-0218-4

Library of Congress Cataloging-in-Publication Data is available.

Manufactured in the United States of America

10   9   8   7   6   5   4   3   2   1

This book is dedicated to
Bruce Duff,
Neill Christie and
Les Enfants de Novembre
N'oublie pas . . .
La vie sans amies
c'est comme un
jardin sans fleurs

Contents

List of Illustrations

Acknowledgements

Writing this book would not have been possible had it not been for the inspiration, criticisms and love of that select group of cherished individuals whom I will always regard as my true family and *autre coeur*.

Barbara, René & Lucette Chevalier, Jacqueline Danno, Hélène Delavault, Marlene Dietrich, Renata & Gottfried Heinwein, Roger Normand, Betty Paillard, Annick Roux, Terry Sanderson, Monica Solash and François & Madeleine Vals. God Bless you all.

Very special thanks to my agent, David Bolt and his wife, Sally. *Chapeau-bas* to a wonderful publishing team: Jeremy Robson, Louise Dixon, Cheryll Roberts, Claudette Byfield, and Dorothy Nicholson.

For their help and contribution to this book, I thank: Jean-Daniel Beauvallet; Peter Burton; David Cavanagh; Murray Chalmers; André Chanut; Neill Christie; Andrew Collins; Adrian Deevoy; Christophe Devos; Ruth Edge; Nicole Garrison; Iestyn George; Dirk van Gils; Andrew Harrison; Martin Hunt; Kanako Ishikawa; Danny Kelly; Kris Kirk; Sandy Lee; Kirsty MacColl; Stuart Maconie; Paul Morley; Christophe Neff; Mark Nevin; Mark Nicholson; Tony Parsons; Keith Porteous-Wood; Manuel Rios-Sastre; Linder Sterling; Martin Talbot; Émmanuel Tellier; Nigel Thomas; Tristan and, finally, Paul Williamson.

Particular thanks go to Bruce Duff, the editor of that excellent Morrissey fanzine, *A Chance to Shine*, and an authority on the subject.

For graciously allowing me access to valuable features and interviews, I thank the editors and staff of the following publications past and present:

Blitz, the *Independent*; *Rage*; *New Musical Express*; *Gay*

Times; *New Zealand Herald*; *Select*; *Details*; *Alternative Press*; *Rock-Sound-Français*; *Best-Français*; *Melody Maker*; *Evening Standard*; *Hot Press*; the *Observer*; *Chicago Tribune*; *Record Mirror*; the *Sunday* and the *Daily Telegraph*; *Les Inrockuptibles*; *The Face*; *Q*; *Him Monthly*; the *Sunday Correspondent*; *Vox*; *Smash Hits* and *Sounds*.

For permission to quote the songs 'Nowhere Fast' (Morrissey–Marr) and 'Interlude' (Georges de la Rue, Hal Shaper), I would like to thank Warner Chappell and EMI Records respectively.

Most important of all, as in the best revues the best acts only come on at the end, I would like to express my thanks, *coeur et âme*, to Steven Patrick Morrissey, and to my wife Jeanne who still is the keeper of my soul.

Morrissey
Landscapes of the Mind

Perdican Reborn

Most of the people who jump onstage and kiss me are male. They're not all young. They're grown, very big men. I can't think of another incident in pop history where men jumped up onstage and kissed a male artist. As to what it is in me that evokes this response, I think I touch on a different passion in people, more romantic than sexual. Singers attract fans with aspects of their own personality. People feel I'm passionate and obsessive. They know this isn't a profession for me. It's a vocation. It's not an egotistical thing but something else. I'm in a dialogue with my audience, and that's something that I need.

Thus spake Steven Patrick Morrissey, former frontman/singer/founder of that most persistently British of institutions, The Smiths. Morrissey, the man who almost single-handedly brought intelligence to contemporary pop.

For more than a decade, Morrissey has conducted a love affair with his public which has become virtually impossible to define. Britain's most articulate singer–songwriter is a complex individual whose lyrics opt for realism, wit mostly of the waspish kind, opinion, asexuality, tension, and love. He prefers not to sanitize, and he has no time for the moon-June trivia which, alarmingly, is churned out with boring regularity by so many of his contemporaries. His voice is haunting and melancholy, that of a man who has experienced every emotion. His songs have at times lent comfort to bedsit solitude through their leanings towards celibacy, vegetarianism, abstinence from alcohol, cigarettes and drugs, and an aversion to most if not all things modern. His heroes are not other singers and the usual confusion of Hollywood glitterati, but socially maligned loners like himself – prime examples being James Dean and Oscar Wilde. His favourite actors are those who made their mark in 'Northern' films such as *Room at the Top* and *Saturday Night and Sunday Morning*.

In May 1984, The Smiths were booked to appear at the Eldorado, the most prestigious of the turn-of-the-century Parisian music-halls. This resulted in a public outcry. Though the group's fans would have been content to listen to their idols standing knee-deep in an Arctic snowstorm, the media voiced very strong disapproval. The Eldorado, whose boards had been graced by such immortals as Piaf, Mistinguett and Chevalier, was about to be invaded by a rowdy pop-audience when the Hippodrome de Pantin, on the northern periphery of the city, specifically catered for such occasions.

Public opinion could not have been more wrong. There was one fleeting moment when Morrissey, in profile in the silvery spotlight, raised his eyes towards the rafters. It was a magical instant which reminded me of the dated but still-potent images which survive on the Pathé newsreels from the period lovingly referred to by the French as 'Les Années Folles'. I was shown the clip of film, and have since studied probably every celluloid frame attributed to The Smiths or Morrissey, but nothing caught my attention quite so much as that totally unexpected initiation into a style of music which hitherto had never interested me. The fact that the revelation came to me via a French stage made the moment that much more poignant. The voice, the stance and facial expression – that final point in quintessentially English beauty which several decades earlier might have inspired lines from a Wilde or a Brooke – coupled with the articulacy of the singer's lyrics and the sheer power of his personality, told me that if as so often is the case the group did not survive the decade, Morrissey certainly would.

Several years later, the Mancunian singer conquered that other bastion of Parisian working-class culture, the Elysée Montmartre. By now he was a solo artiste with two hit albums tucked under his belt, and promoting a third in a brief but gruelling tour of Europe. One of his new songs, intentionally plaintive, was 'Will Never Marry'. It brought him considerable acclaim, and drafted a multitude of new recruits to his cult. It also quite likely summed him up more than anything he had done before, particularly when he proclaimed, 'I will live my life as I will undoubtedly die – alone'.

My first 'live' experience of Morrissey, on 11 December 1992, was one that I will doubtless not forget. Mindless of the pouring rain, the faithful had congregated outside the Sheffield City Hall for more than two hours, hoping to catch a glimpse of the man they affectionately called Mozzer dashing into the theatre via a side-entrance. Plastered-down quiffs and soaked, transparent Arsenal T-shirts were in abundance and there was only one umbrella in sight to ward off the deluge – mine. The average age of these mostly male (and I am told heterosexual) admirers could not have exceeded twenty. Many carried flowers, protruding from their back pockets in imitation of Morrissey. The city's florists had that day boasted record sales. Many had sold out of daffodils within moments of raising their shutters, and these blooms were hurled like missiles the instant the singer stepped on to the stage, following the excruciating Klaus Nomi overture and the chanting of Morrissey's name to the 'Here We Go!' football anthem which had shaken the City Hall's foundations.

The young woman sitting next to my wife all but propelled herself over the balcony railings, whilst her escort buried his head into his hands and wept inconsolably throughout the first three songs. I too felt a lump come to my throat. This man had a real, heart-stirring talent. Whipping the microphone chord with frenetic abandon during several hard-rock numbers, he did all he could to encourage the

body-swimmers – the bravest of the fans who were passed
over the heads of the others by a succession of hands, their
sole aim to negotiate the four-foot drop into the orchestra
pit, outsmart the bouncers, and hug their man. In tender
moments, Morrissey perched precariously on one of the
monitors, reaching out to touch sweaty hands and running
the risk of being hauled into the mêlée of gyrating bodies –
and all the while disproving the tenet that big, stiff-upper-
lipped Englishmen cannot express emotion by shedding a
tear or two.

Outside the theatre after the show, as if by magic, it had
stopped raining and the faithful were parading their battle-
spoils – fragments of the glass from which Morrissey had
sipped his Perrier water, mushy flowers which he had thrown
back to them . . . and a large piece of lamé shirt which, its
new owner proclaimed, would spend the rest of the night
next to her heart. I had witnessed recitals by some of the
most legendary figures in showbusiness, homegrown and
international, but never before had I seen devotion quite like
this.

No longer adolescent, but still essentially the loner, Steven
Patrick Morrissey is neither pop star nor rock idol. He cannot adequately be slotted into any particular pigeon-hole,
and nor should he be for he is now accessible to a wider,
more reverent and hypercritical public than any of his predecessors. At the mere mention of his name, most music
publications vacillate between censure and praise, yet few
may ignore him. In spite of this incessant attention he
remains aloof, mysterious, enigmatic and reclusive – a philosophical, witty, ironic, hard-hitting individual who is one of
his country's essential communicators, a living link between
Victorian literary ideals and modern-day bedsit drama. He is
the uncrowned, undisputed champion of some of the more
complex aspects of the human condition, and as such quite
possibly the most influential entertainer of his generation.

1

Born Old, Sadly Wise . . .

Steven Patrick Morrissey was born at the Davyhulme Park Hospital, Manchester, on 22 May 1959, the second child of Peter Morrissey and his wife Elizabeth (née Dwyer) who had emigrated to England from their native Dublin several years before. Home, for the first ten years of his life, was 17 Harper Street, in the, Hulme district of the city which, in common with most of North-West England, was undergoing a period of changes and mixed emotions, particularly within the artistic world. Films like *A Taste of Honey*, *Saturday Night and Sunday Morning* and *The L-Shaped Room*, with their controversial plots and gritty dialogue, were about to take the country by storm. *Coronation Street*, in its pre-Cosmopolitan era, would soon top the television ratings and, as the young Morrissey was beginning his education at St Wilfred's Primary School, Manchester was playing Liverpool at its own game by coming forward with a string of entertainers, adding lustre to those all-powerful pop charts: Herman's Hermits, Freddie and The Dreamers, Wayne Fontana and The Mindbenders – contracted with Kennedy Street Enterprises – gave The Beatles a run for their money not just in Britain, but worldwide.

At the end of 1965, however, Manchester was witness to a kind of infamy it could have done without: the so-called Moors Murders perpetrated by Ian Brady and Myra Hindley – the former a Glaswegian who had recently relocated to Moss Side, an aficionado of Hitler and the crazed writings of the Marquis de Sade; the latter his lover, and arguably one of the most evil women in British criminal history.

Brady and Hindley were shut away for life at around the time of Morrissey's seventh birthday, and even with newspaper reports in those days much less graphic than they would have been today it is not difficult to assess the effect these horrific slayings would have had on the mind of an impressionable child, as in fact they had on an entire generation of Northerners, myself included. He was already prone to nightmares, the first occurring when he was six, after he had stayed up to watch an episode of the television series, *Tales of Mystery and Imagination*. The Brady-Hindley horror, of course, was disturbingly real.

The Smiths' 1984 song, 'Suffer Little Children' referred to the murdered youngsters – John Kilbride, Edward Evans and Lesley Ann Downey – by name, and was complemented and thus made more realistic by the addition of mocking laughter, an imitation of Hindley's own. The British media by and large, unlike their European counterparts, were not quite ready for this particular brand of realism – precedents set in the form of dramatic songs by Edith Piaf ('L'homme à la moto'), the Shangri-Las ('Leader of the Pack') and the British songstress Twinkle ('Terry') had been met with fierce criticism – and some sections of the media attacked the song as 'sick', though it had never been The Smiths' intention to offend. The pastiche also reminded us, lest we should forget, 'But fresh lilaced moorland fields cannot hide the stolid stench of death', and concluded that Manchester really did have something to answer for.

Morrissey remembered Manchester in the sixties as being very violent, explaining that one afternoon at a Stretford fair, he had been punched by a thug for no apparent reason other than that he had been standing there at the time. He added, 'You just accepted it. There never had to be any reason.' He admitted too that his remaining years at school were not always happy, though they were tolerable . . . and they did of course help to sow the seed for his eventual career.

A major land-clearance operation resulted in the Morrissey family being transferred to a council house at 384 Kings Road, in Stretford, and in 1970 Morrissey moved up to the nearby St Mary's Secondary Modern. This was a tough, Spartan establishment run by a military-orientated headmaster named Vincent Morgan – a man who like many of his contemporaries was firmly in favour of the adage 'Spare the rod and spoil the child', though one would scarcely believe that discipline really went as far as the knee in the groin or the elbow in the face, as in the song.

'I can remember being forcibly kicked by the PE teacher. I'd taken the ball off him,' Morrissey later recalled. 'His response was to ignore the game, ignore the ball, ignore the pupils and just kick me. I stood quite still.' As in any stalwart Catholic household, the discussion of sex and the use of strong language were never on the agenda. 'I was raised with the notion that excitement, exuberance and extremities were for other people, and not for me,' he said, and remembered his one and only sex education lesson, delivered by a Mr Thomas – 'a very gung-ho rugby type' – who admonished, 'You know penis? Well, it's your dick. What more do you want to know?'

Though he hated school and to all intents stuck it out because of his passion for sport – in particular, long-distance running – Morrissey nurtured a passion for writing from a tender age. He told Jean-Daniel Beauvallet of *Les Inrockuptibles*:

I began writing when I was six. It was the only natural thing to do. I wrote whilst sitting on the toilet, and I always had a plank across the bath for my books, pens and papers ... I was *never* separated from my books and pens and I could never sleep without piles of books next to my bed. What I wrote was immaterial, though being able to write was probably better than having friends.

Miserable, no doubt, and probably disillusioned with his lot in life, Morrissey searched for ultimate inspiration not amongst schoolfriends and those close to him, but from long-dead heroes. When asked if his affinity for James Dean was more than mere admiration, he replied, 'Profoundly more. James Dean was much more than the actor in *Rebel Without a Cause*. He was a great symbol. There was nothing that remarkable about his acting in my opinion, but he always seemed to be in control of every situation. People like that are only too rare. The man's entire life was so wonderfully perfect.'

Morrissey applauded the sadness of Billy Fury who had always wanted to be a rock star, but who had found lasting fame with tender ballads such as 'Halfway to Paradise'. He clung to the sharp, Lancastrian humour of George Formby, Jimmy Clitheroe and Gracie Fields. His mother, a librarian, later introduced him to the works of the maligned genius Oscar Wilde, of whom he said, 'As I blundered through my late teens I was quite isolated. In a way he became a companion, and as I get older, the adoration increases. I'm never without him. It's almost biblical, like carrying your rosary around with you. He had a life that was really tragic, yet it's curious that he was so witty.'

At the age of six, Morrissey purchased his first 7-inch vinyl singles: Marianne Faithfull's 'Come And Stay With Me' and sultry French star Françoise Hardy's 'Another Place'. Thereafter he developed a passion for Sandie Shaw, Dusty Springfield and Twinkle. He became a fan of Nico, the ill-fated British singer with the The Velvet Underground, buying her *Chelsea Girl* and *Desert Shore* albums. 'I was extremely comforted by her isolation and depression,' he said. 1970, however, saw the emergence of glam-rock with its garish clothes, tank-tops, painted faces, platform shoes, and outspoken, effiminate-looking and often bisexual frontmen such as David Bowie and Marc Bolan of T Rex. Over the course of the next few years he would see both these artists, along with Mott The Hoople and Roxy Music, at the King's Hall in the Manchester suburb of Belle Vue.

None of these people, however, influenced Morrissey quite so profoundly as The New York Dolls, arguably the most outrageous act of the entire glam-rock proto-punk era. The Dolls had been formed in 1972, and soon afterwards their drummer had been found dead in a Chelsea bathtub. Another founder member, the guitarist Johnny Thunders, broke away from the group in 1975 to front another perennial Morrissey favourite, The Heartbreakers, and survive countless drugs/drink-orientated binges until April 1991, when, at thirty-eight, he was found lifeless in a New Orleans hotel room. Jerry Nolan, The Dolls' replacement drummer, struggled on for nine months before succumbing to a stroke. Morrissey saw the group on *The Old Grey Whistle Test* in 1973, when they were at their tacky prime, promoting their debut album produced by guitar virtuoso Todd Rundgren. 'I was thirteen. It was my very first emotional experience,' he enthused. 'The next day I became twenty-nine. But being devoted to The Dolls ruined my education. The teachers expected me to turn up for maths in drag!'

Morrissey, in the time-honoured tradition of most loners both spiritually and artistically different from the others in his class at St Mary's, rapidly found release in this new-found, controversial form of hero-worship. He recalled, 'I loved these people. I gave them my life, my youth. Beyond the perimeter of pop music there was a drop at the edge of the world. When young I instantly excluded the human race in favour of pop music. Music is like a drug, but there are no rehabilitation centres.'

Another inspiration around this time was the American group Sparks, fronted by a tall, pencil-thin individual named Ron Mael with sleeked-back hair, starting eyes and Hitlerian moustache. Their song, 'This Town Ain't Big

Enough for the Both of Us', sung by Mael's brother, Russ, in an ear-splitting falsetto, topped the British hit-parade early in 1974 and gave way to their hit album, *Kimono My House* – the title being a pun on the old Rosemary Clooney number. Morrissey liked the album so much that he wrote an audaciously praising letter, the first of many, to the *New Musical Express*. Not only was the letter published, it received a personal reply from the letters editor, describing Morrissey's missive in such a way as would have impressed every one of his literary champions:

> Conviction oozes from every sentence like the very ichor of life itself from the metal life-support systems of the Bronze Giant of Fangorak. The eyes of Mr Morrissey gleam with a missionary zeal that shames into submission the cringing doubts of those yet unconvinced.

This was a justifiable reward – one of recognition – which made up for Morrissey's rejection letter from Lesley Duxbury, then the producer of *Coronation Street*. He told *Smash Hits* several years later, 'My scripts were probably a little too adventurous for *The Street*. The best one had them planting a jukebox in The Rovers. Naturally, these storylines were rejected . . . there were a couple of divorces in there and the odd strangulation!'

Morrissey left school in July 1975, having acquired no formal qualifications. To remedy this he enrolled on a one-year course with Stretford Technical College – this would ensure him GCE O Levels in English Literature, Sociology and the General Paper. Music, however, was still his greatest preoccupation. Listening to records took up most of his leisure time. He became sufficiently interested in The Sex Pistols – their mentor, Malcolm McLaren, had for a brief period managed The New York Dolls – to write a letter to the *New Musical Express*. Coloured with no small amount of the biting, sarcastic wit which would later become recognized as a feature of his work, he wished The Sex Pistols lasting fame, explaining, '. . . then they will be able to afford some new clothes which don't look as though they've been slept in.' Morrissey, along with many other musical hopefuls in an age when success, by and large, had nothing to do with talent, witnessed the group's Manchester debut at the Lesser Free Trade Hall in June 1976. Though he recorded at the time that it had been 'an exciting and magical experience', on later reflection he changed his mind, saying, 'It was a dank night that only history has given a little colour to.'

Whilst awaiting his exam results, Morrissey visited an aunt in New Jersey, his first trip to the United States. The country was then gripped in the 'Coma Girl' affair – a young woman named Karen Quinlan, who had lain unconscious for more than a year, was, after a great deal of deliberation and wrangling between the courts, the media and innumerable religious groups, taken to a nursing home where her treatment was stopped, enabling her to die 'naturally and peacefully'. Almost certainly, the effect this had on the sixteen-years-old Stretford youth inspired 'Girlfriend in a Coma', one of his most moving works.

In common with many school-leavers at the time, unable to find suitable employment Morrissey joined the dole queue, though a lack of funds did not prevent him from scrimping and saving in order to see some of his idols in concert. One of these was the American punk poet, Patti Smith, whose big hit at the time was the album *Horses*. Morrissey wrote a letter to *Sounds*, arguing that the album showed 'more potential than just about any other release in recent memory', and he travelled all the way to Birmingham to see her show. A few weeks later, he attacked *Sounds* because one of the publication's more prominent reviewers, John Ingham, had severely criticized The New York Dolls. Ingham was told, in no uncertain terms, to 'stick with The Sex Pistols, whose infantile approach and nondescript music will no doubt match your intelligence'. Another letter, published in the *New Musical Express*, concerning its apparent neglect of that other Manchester quartet, The Buzzcocks, was even more frank and illuminating.

> Buzzcocks differ in only one way from their contemporaries: they possess a spark of originality. Their music gives you the impression they spent longer than the customary ten minutes clutching the quill in preparation to write . . . and in these dark days when Patti Smith, Loudon Wainwright or even The New York Dolls fail to make any impact on Radio 1 DJs, common sense is therefore not so common. Go and see them first and then you may have the audacity to contradict me, you stupid sluts.

Morrissey was no doubt amused by the editor's lengthy reply which, after promising that a piece on the Buzzcocks was on the stocks, ended with: 'Now go away, you nasty little brat!'

Early in 1977 Morrissey began working as a clerk for the Inland Revenue, a move which he later said had only added to his misery and disenchantment with the world.

Over the next few months, Morrissey coped with his 'career' – and no doubt came to terms with his parents' recent divorce – by spending most of his spare time planning a literary future. More concerts were attended, in and around Manchester – Blondie, Talking Heads and The Ramones offered a light at the end of the tunnel. A fervent anti-royalist, he was doubtless cheered up by the latest, shocking exploits of The Sex Pistols. In June 1977, the Queen celebrated her Silver Jubilee with mass pageantry and street parties up and down the country – and The Sex Pistols' highly irreverent 'God Save The Queen' reached the top of the British hit parade. To add insult to injury, Malcolm McLaren hosted a boat party in the middle of the Thames, smack in front of the Houses of Parliament, and hundreds of fans turned up for the bash . . . sporting T-shirts depicting their sovereign wearing a safety-pin through her nose. During the ensuing riot, several of the group's entourage suffered serious injury. The group themselves were temporarily forced into hiding. Morrissey is alleged to have participated in an anti-royal demonstration, waving a banner which proclaimed: BAN THE JUBILEE.

Eight years later the singer would publicly air his aversions by saying, 'I despise royalty. It's fairy-story nonsense, the very idea of their existence in these days when people are dying because they don't have enough money to operate one radiator in the house. It's immoral!' The statement would be complemented by the brutally frank second stanza of 'Nowhere Fast'.

> I'd like to drop my trousers to the Queen
> Every sensible child will know what this means
> The poor and the needy
> Are selfish and greedy on her terms.

Morrissey had for some time been corresponding with a young, aspiring guitarist from Wythenshawe named Billy Duffy, and in November 1977 the pair met. Duffy, an ardent New York Dolls fan, had been asked to augment what was left of the recently split Nosebleeds, and having already been knocked sideways by Morrissey's articulate lyrics – in particular 'I Think I'm Ready for the Electric Chair' – he suggested that Morrissey should be engaged as the group's new vocalist.

The Nosebleeds – formerly Wild Ram, then Ed Banger and The Nosebleeds – had been formed during the early seventies by a singing milkman named Eddie Garrity (of no relation to that other singing milkman who fronted Freddie and the Dreamers). Their bass player was Pete Crookes, Toby (Philip Tolman) was their drummer, and completing the line-up was Vini Reilly, the guitarist who later played on Morrissey's first solo album.

Such was Morrissey's authority on the Manchester music-scene that he was invited to contribute articles to the Southern-based fanzine, *Kids Stuff*. This venture afforded him access to a Patti Smith press conference in London in March 1978, from which he doubtless drew considerable inspiration for his work with The Nosebleeds, whose stage debut at the Manchester Polytechnic had been pencilled in for 15 April. Morrissey's 'confrontation' with the lady herself, however, left him decidedly unimpressed, as he later recollected, 'She farted four times . . . and the room was crowded with young, impressionable people. There was one boy at the front who was no more than seventeen. She walked up to him . . . and loudly asked him an extremely vulgar question about how sexually endowed he was. I think she was completely mad at the time. The lesson here is that sometimes it's best to cherish your illusions about people you admire than it is to meet them.'

At around this time, Morrissey dashed off another florid letter to the *New Musical Express* in praise of Johnny Thunders and The Heartbreakers, whom he claimed were 'newer than the New Wave and (surprise) they *can* play!' His letter ended with the postscript, 'I work for the Inland Revenue – am I still allowed to be a punk?' Equally quick off the mark was the editor's reply, 'You lie. . . you work for Johnny Thunders and The Heartbreakers!' Upon his return to base, Morrissey gave up his job with the Inland Revenue to pursue his musical calling.

The Nosebleeds appeared on the same bill as several regional groups, virtually all of them unknown. The songs, Morrissey-Duffy collaborations, were, according to contemporary reports, well received, and included 'I Think I'm Ready For The Electric Chair', 'I Get Nervous', and 'Peppermint Heaven'. A few weeks later, the group supported Magazine, at the Manchester Ritz. Halfway through their set there was a brief power-cut which Morrissey overcame with comparative ease, and during 'Peppermint Heaven' he flung sweets into the audience, a gesture which was appreciated, as was his and Billy Duffy's arrangement of the Shangri-Las' 'Give Him a Great Big Kiss', for which they had effected no change of gender. Paul Morley, then writing for the *New Musical Express*, reported that 'Steven Morrissey has charisma'. Sadly, soon afterwards the group split up. Billy Duffy teamed up with Slaughter and the Dogs. Morrissey returned to sign on at the labour exchange.

In November 1978, Morrissey was nevertheless able to afford to fly out to Colorado – the aunt he had visited in New Jersey had recently relocated. The break offered him pause for thought wherein, obviously aware of his potential, he was able to speculate about his future. For the time being, this amounted to no more than working behind the counter in a Manchester record shop, though he was still fervently dispatching letters and reviews to the music press. One, comparing The Police to his favourite but lesser known The Cramps, boldly dismissed the former as 'a great big sloppy bowl of mush'.

Perhaps Morrissey's closest friend at this time – and just as important today as she was then – was the young artist Linder (Linda Mulvey/Linder Sterling), born in Liverpool in 1954, and in those days one of the celebrities of Whalley Range, the area of Manchester known as 'the home of the bedsit' (and some years later referred to in the song 'Miserable Lie'). Linder was a member of the punk-jazz group Ludus, who also featured Toby, the drummer from The Nosebleeds. The group had played successful engagements in some of the country's larger concert halls, including the Hammersmith Odeon. Ludus' experimental debut 12-inch EP, *The Visit*, was released in March 1980 on the Hormones label, and featured such evocative titles as 'I Can't Swim, I Have Nightmares'. Linder and Morrissey have, and rightfully so, kept their friendship free from media scrutiny and perhaps more than anyone this young woman was able to reach and comprehend the Stretford bard's inner psyche as the pair searched for artistic and spiritual inspiration amongst the dark, deserted backstreets of Manchester, or alternatively within the peaceful confines of West Didsbury's iron-gated Southern Cemetery. There was nothing whatsoever morbid about this. Oscar Wilde, Chopin and Colette had all searched amongst the dilapidated tombstones of Paris's Père Lachaise Cemetery 'to find themselves', and having done so had ultimately decided to be buried there. A few years ago, on one of my bi-annual visits to Edith Piaf's grave at the Père Lachaise, I was not surprised to discover, written in thick black felt-tip across the plinth of Oscar Wilde's Jacob Epstein tomb: OSCAR AND MORRISSEY ARE GOD. These excursions with Linder also inspired the song 'Cemetry Gates', deliberately misspelt by Morrissey in a moment's amusement.

Early in 1980, Morrissey followed in the recent footsteps of his father when he took a job as a hospital porter. However, when a superior asked him to clean the surgeons' bloodstained white uniforms, he disapproved and left. Once again he turned most of his attention to writing letters to the music press, becoming unofficial Manchester correspondent for *Record Mirror*. After seeing the Cramps at the Polytechnic, he enthused, 'They are the most *beautiful* group I've ever seen . . . Manchester will never be the same again!' Ludus' performance at the Beach Club was similarly lauded when he wrote of Linder's 'wild mélange of ill-disciplined and extraneous vocal movements'.

The Beach Club was run by Tony Wilson, the former presenter with the news programme *Granada Reports*, and the head of the acclaimed independent Factory Records, whose 'golden boys', Joy Division, had recently been devastated by the death of their frontman-singer, Ian Curtis. This handsome, despondent young man had ultimately decided to make an exit from society by taking a penknife and carving a smile on his face, before hanging himself; Manchester's entertainment industry was to take years to recover from the tragedy. Morrissey was unenthusiastic about the ensemble and commented, 'I saw them just before "the death", and I was astonishingly unmoved, as were the audience.'

For his part Tony Wilson was suitably impressed with Morrissey's lyrics and prose, and several years later claimed to have seen a one-act play written by Morrissey. Proclaiming Morrissey a potential 'Jeanette Winterson of the Eighties', he added insult to injury by saying, 'He's a woman in a man's body – she's a man in a woman's body.' Morrissey was cut deeply by the remark, and angrily hit back, 'He's a PIG trapped inside a man's body . . . the day somebody shoves Wilson into the boot of a car and drives his body out to Saddleworth Moor, that's the day Manchester music will be revived.' Later, he complained that the first part of his statement had been misquoted, adding, 'What I really said was that he is a man trapped inside a pig's body.'

Most appropriately, Morrissey's talent for Wildean sallies was brought to the attention of John Muir, the director of the Manchester-based *Babylon Books*, and this time the end result was considerably more than a handful of paragraphs printed in the already opinionated music press. Morrissey's fascination for The New York Dolls resulted in a compelling, 24-page booklet which Muir published in 1981. The biography, which contained over forty photographs of the group, including Morrissey's own – and an acknowledgement which included the words, 'Many thanks to Steven Morrissey – watch out for his James Dean book' – sold in excess of 3,000 copies, in those days a figure not readily achieved by many mainstream pop publishers. Morrissey proclaimed, 'The New York Dolls were my private "Heartbreak Hotel" . . . as important to me as Elvis Presley was to the entire language of rock and roll.' Needless to say, Muir encouraged him to complete his biography of Dean as quickly as possible.

In July 1980, Morrissey witnessed a performance by the gender-bender punk-star Iggy Pop at the Manchester Apollo. He was not impressed and with caustic abandon reported in *Record Mirror*, 'One would imagine that the next step for him would be retirement.' As a pop journalist, however, he was coming to the end of his particular road, though what he probably did not know was that he was about to take the first steps on a trail towards an adventure which would transform his entire life – a journey which would culminate with his becoming greater and considerably more revered than any of his contemporaries, or any of the artistes he had written about . . .

2

A Combined Body of Mancunians

Like Rodgers and Hart, Leiber and Stoller, Jagger and Richard, Lennon and McCartney, and Simon and Garfunkel, before them, the seemingly unlikely partnership of Morrissey and Marr influenced an entire generation. Their pairing epitomized a previously unexplored world of adolescent drama, Northern streets and back-to-back houses, angst, and bedsit blues in general. Not enough may be said as to their importance. Two young men, ensconced in the same city yet ostensibly a world apart, sharing the same dreams and ideals, and the same manic obsession to succeed. In short, they *had* to meet.

John Martin Maher was born 31 October 1963 at Chorlton-on-Medlock, the eldest child of Irish immigrants who had settled in the Ardwick district of Manchester during the early sixties, moving to Wythenshawe in 1973. Educationally, Maher was given a considerable advantage over his future partner. He attended St Augustine's Grammar School, though he did not fare quite so well, and failed to acquire the same intellectual standing. And if he at least set down his guitar long enough to kick around a football – displaying ample talent to play for the Manchester Boys and be offered a trial for Manchester City – music and only music ruled the youngster's life, leaving little time for other pursuits, or for the gleaning of those real life experiences and compassion for the world which Morrissey was already wearing like a second skin. The first record Maher bought was T Rex's 'Jeepster'. His first pop concert, Rod Stewart and The Faces at Belle Vue in 1974. In a recent rare interview he confided that his life had unfolded like a musician's fairy-tale, adding, 'I was one of those kids who always got the plastic guitar at Christmas. Everybody knew me as "that cunt who walks around with a guitar case who thinks he's gonna be a big success". I developed a very thick skin.'

At St Augustine's Maher – almost a guitar virtuoso by the age of twelve, and an ' essential fan' of Patti Smith and The New York Dolls – quickly gathered a clique of musical hopefuls about him. He is said to have been outspoken, cocky, and always sure of himself. One of his best friends was Andy Rourke, a reserved-on-the-surface, long-haired youth from Ashton-upon-Mersey who, it later transpired, was already experimenting with soft drugs. Rourke and Maher were in the same class at school. They talked incessantly about pop music, played truant a lot, and, away from school, were virtually inseperable, spending a lot of time at Rourke's house emulating the styles and joining in with the recordings of Marc Bolan, Nils Lofgren, Keith Richard and their arch-hero, Rory Gallagher – Maher on guitar or harmonica, Rourke on acoustic guitar.

Very soon, Maher and Rourke began playing on a regular basis at their local youth club, and at the beginning of 1977 formed The Paris Valentinos with two slightly older school pals: Kevin Williams on vocals/bass, and Bobby Durkin – who had auditioned for the Manchester Youth Orchestra, been granted a scholarship, and subsequently dropped out – on drums. Unable to afford beer and spirits they tried to live up to their rock-band image by guzzling cheap cider.

The Paris Valentinos made their début at a Benchill street-party later that year, covering the noisiest songs in the repertoires of Gallagher, Thin Lizzy and Tom Petty; by way of a sympathetic priest they were invited to perform at their local church's Folk Masses. But Maher was only ever interested in being a serious musician with a *real* group playing *real* venues – it is incredible that he was still only fourteen – and The Paris Valentinos suffered an early demise. Though he

and Rourke would stay together off-and-on until the forma-
tion of The Smiths, with Durkin hovering conveniently in
the background waiting for an opportunity to better himself,
Kevin Williams later pursued a theatrical career, changed his
surname to Kennedy, and plays the hapless intellectual dust-
man-turned-supermarket executive Curly Watts in
Coronation Street.

After The Paris Valentinos, Maher played briefly with
Sister Ray, a rough-and-ready ensemble who achieved minor
acclaim early in 1979 at the Wythenshawe Forum. His next
venture was with White Dice, formed by Paul Whittall and
the keyboards player Rob Allman at the end of 1979, re-
recruiting the services of Durkin and Rourke. The future of
the new group seemed promising. Within weeks they had put
together a demo-tape on a portable machine and dispatched
it to the talent scout Jake Riviera, of London's F-Beat
Records. The song, Allman and Maher's 'Someone Waved
Goodbye', earned them an audition in April 1980, and they
spent some time perfecting and recording several other numbers, all penned by Allman and Maher, though in the end
Riviera turned them down. For a while, Durkin dropped out
of the group and was replaced by Craig Mitchell, and Maher
attempted to appease his parents by enrolling at
Wythenshawe College and studying for his O Levels. Too
preoccupied with his guitar and his girlfriend, Angela, whom
he would later marry, he set off in search of new horizons,
forfeiting his education *and* White Dice. A new group,
Freaky Party, was formed but never really got off the
ground, and to make ends meet he found employment as a
sales assistant at X Clothes, an off-beat fashion shop on
Chapel Walks.

Inspiration came in the shape of two new friends, Matt
Johnson and Joe Moss. Johnson, the vocalist with The The,
was introduced to him by Pete Hunt, the manager of an
Altrincham record store. Maher had left his parents' council
home and was living in the district at the home of Granada

Television producer Shelley Rohde, who had provided him
and his musician friends with a sound-proofed attic for
rehearsals. Maher came close to joining The The – eventually, of course, he would, but at the time a mutual shortage
of funds coupled with the group's being based in London
made regular travel up and down the country impossible.
Johnson, however, would remain both close friend and
guide.

Joe Moss was the rag-trade baron who had established his
name selling sandals during the late sixties, before progress-
ing to wholesale jeans. He had opened a small chain of shops
named Crazy Face, one of which was situated near X
Clothes in Chapel Walks, and, no mean guitarist himself, he
soon learned of the talented youngster on his doorstep. Such
was his enthusiasm once he had heard Maher play that he
promised to back any would-be group he might come up
with. Maher's confidence and talent were such that he knew
he could virtually have the pick of the best young musicians
in Manchester, but what he sorely lacked was a competent
vocalist/lyricist.

Some years before, Billy Duffy had shown Maher a sheaf
of lyrics which Morrissey had written for The Nosebleeds,
but it seems that Duffy was now unable or unwilling to fur-
nish Maher with an introduction. Years later, after Duffy
had joined The Cult, he said, 'Morrissey hated me because
he thought we'd stolen lyrics from him, which we probably
had.' Maher therefore contacted another mutual friend, a
musician named Steve Pomfret, who gave him Morrissey's
address – with the warning that the young poet was not
always easy to approach. After some deliberation, the loquacious guitarist opted to extract a leaf out of Jerry Leiber's
book. Leiber and Stoller, the great American songwriting
team of the late fifties, had turned out a string of million-sell-
ers for artistes as diverse as Elvis Presley, Peggy Lee, Edith
Piaf, and The Drifters. Mike Stoller has often repeated the
anecdote of how, one morning, he had opened his door to

find Leiber standing on the mat with the announcement, 'Hi! Why don't we start doing songs together?'

In retrospect, bearing in mind that neither Morrissey nor Maher was known outside Manchester, their Livingstone-Stanley meeting does seem the substance of which dreams are made, though this only makes what happened next more remarkable and, one has to say, poetically romantic. Maher, with his X Clothes garb, gift-of-the-gab and late-fifties hair-style must have been as much of a shock to Morrissey as the bespectacled, lanky Stretford bard must have been to him. Also, one is given the impression that the slight, angelic-looking Maher may have been initially afraid of the bigger, no doubt tougher Morrissey – not physical fear, exactly, but the fear of being rejected when he must have been hoping to glean so much from this first encounter – which is possibly why he spouted, with added cockiness, 'This is how Leiber and Stoller met. I know who *you* are. I'm a fabulous guitar player and I'm interested in forming a group. Let me in!' All which probably reflects the Morrissey aura, even then, and which brought the simple response: 'What kind of music do you like?', thus enabling these two very different personages to get on like the proverbial house on fire, at once and with the minimum of reserve.

Morrissey described this meeting with typical irony: 'Johnny came up and pressed his nose against the window . . . it left a terrible smudge. I think he'd been eating choco-late. He seemed terribly sure of what he wanted to do, which I liked. He said, "Let's do it, and do it now!" So we did it! Then!"

The day after this histrionic rencontre, Morrissey and Maher collaborated on their first two songs. 'The Hand that Rocks the Cradle' – a title which had been used as far back as 1917 for an American newsreel documentary about con-traception – told of childhood nightmares brought about by dark, terrifying bedroom shapes, a theme which had also inspired a series of British child-behaviour shorts in the early forties, to which Marr's brilliantly evocative refrains would not have been out of place. 'Suffer Little Children' was a phrase much in use at the time. The *Sunday Times* had recently run a feature on Myra Hindley under the heading 'The Woman Who Cannot Face The Truth', in which it was claimed that each time the hard-faced killer ventured forth from her cell, her fellow inmates chanted, 'Suffer little children to come unto me . . .' Morrissey's poignant lyrics – he referred to each of the murdered children by name and even spoke tenderly of the white necklace that Lesley-Anne Downey had been wearing at the time of her death – would later get him into trouble.

Both these songs were put on to demo-tapes at Decibel Studios, with Maher on guitar, Simon Wolstencroft (formerly of Freaky Party) on drums, and the recording engineer, Dale, filling in on bass. From then on, the pace speeded considerably: Morrissey, with a seemingly endless mental store of ideas, images and anecdotes, set everything down on paper, and Maher organized the group's first engagement, though in effect there was no 'group' – Dale had only played for the demo session as a favour, and Wolstencroft was apparently uninterested in working full time with any group, least of all one headed by Morrissey and Maher, who quite clearly were prepared to settle for nothing less than perfection. Eventually, a date was settled with the promoters of a fashion show at the Ritz, supporting the glamorous-sounding Blue Rondo a La Turk, a ten-piece band, very much in vogue, steeped in the traditions of salsa and jazz. Their latest album, *Chewing the Fat*, had been part-produced by Clive Langer, who later worked with Morrissey when Morrissey turned solo. The pair then began their search for two young, suitably accomplished – and, most important of all, compatible – musicians to complete their line-up.

Recruiting financial aid and backing from a reputable record company proved the ultimate challenge – when none was forthcoming locally, Maher travelled to London, cutting down on expenses by sleeping on the floor in Matt Johnson's flat. Morrissey, meanwhile, had taken the all-important step of dispensing with his Christian names, on the premise that, as history had proved so often, any poet worthy of his salt was only ever remembered by his surname. He said, 'The thing was that I was always getting called Steve – and I was never a Steve. I thought, well, I only need one name anyway . . . these days I only hear the name from strangers, as a term of supposed intimacy.'

It was Morrissey who chose the name for his group. Whilst many bands were trying to dazzle their fans by exotic, often incomprehensible and ludicrous names, he made a play for the plain and selected a nomenclature which would be readily associated with his basic Northern upbringing – The Smiths. He told the press, 'This is real music played by real people. The Smiths are absolutely real faces instead of the frills, the gloss and the pantomime popular music has become immersed in. There is no human element in anything any more, and I think The Smiths reintroduce that quite firmly. There's no façade. We're simply there to be seen as real people.'

Morrissey was anxious that the companions of his adventure should follow his sanitized lead. The New York Dolls, Joy Division, the Rolling Stones and other pioneer groups had lost members through drugs and debauchery. Janis Joplin, Jimi Hendrix and Jim Morrison had burned themselves out before the age of thirty, creating mayhem and confusion amongst their disciples. The Smiths would therefore be anti-drug and violence, anti-authority whilst authoritative on human issues, intelligent, pro-Northern and free from vice. Had the young man known of his group's past and present drug-taking, its eventual line-up almost certainly would not have been the same, for he himself had never so much as smoked a cigarette.

The first member of the group to be recruited was the drummer, Mike Joyce. A few months older than Maher, the

Fallowfield youth had while still at school played for the punk-based group The Hoax, in regional pubs and clubs, and once at Manchester Polytechnic. Upon their demise he had played for Victim (whose single, 'Why are Fire Engines Red?', had had a sleeve designed by Linder). His audition for The Smiths took place at Spirit Studios, prior to which he is alleged to have eaten magic mushrooms, playing so frantically as a result of his hallucinations that he felt certain he would not be engaged. Morrissey and Maher were so astonished at the way he tackled their new song, 'What Difference Does it Make?', that they probably did not realize what Joyce had done. He was taken on, and a few days later Victim folded.

Thanks to Morrissey's surprise decision to bring in his old schoolfriend James Maker – claimed by some to have been the spitting image of his idol, James Dean – as Master of Ceremonies and go-go dancer, The Smiths' début, at the Ritz on 4 October 1982, was nothing less than an eye-opener. Maker, wearing an early-sixties-style suit and high-heeled shoes, introduced the group to the 300-plus audience in near-perfect French. During the brief spot of just three songs, exceptionally well-received, he writhed and danced energetically, alternating between playing the maracas and tambourine. Unable to locate a full-time bass guitarist in time for the show, Maher had persuaded Dale of Decibel Studios to fill in, and another friend stood in on acoustic guitar. The group hit a snag when, halfway through 'The Hand that Rocks the Cradle', Mike Joyce injected too much enthusiasm into his playing and burst a drum-skin, a problem which he dealt with by turning the drum upside-down. Then, after 'Suffer Little Children' came 'Handsome Devil', with its cleverly ambiguous lyrics.

This song brought condemnation from some sources and instant approval from the gay community. The audacity of one line – 'Let me get my hands on your mammary glands' – coupled with the harsh directness of 'And when we're in your scholarly room / Who will swallow whom?' raised the obvious questions from the media, most of whom had confused the singer/situation in the way their predecessors had confused the actor/interpretations of Hollywood legends during the thirties and forties. Morrissey was suitably responsive, saying, 'If you glance over my words briefly, I suppose some suggestions *do* come to the fore.' This, linked with the singer's absolute reluctance to discuss his personal life – the media's assumption being that if one insists upon privacy, one must have something to hide – only made his and The Smiths' presence on the music-scene that much more exciting.

Within weeks of their Ritz début, The Smiths failed to gain two potentially valuable recording contracts. Their demo-tapes had been scrutinized by the music publishers Bryan Morrison and Dick Leahy (Morrison had managed The Pretty Things, and during the Walker Brothers/Dusty Springfield recording boom of the sixties Leahy had worked for Philips, before becoming managing director of Bell Records), but they were turned down in favour of Wham!. At this point they were approached by Joe Moss who, under constant pressure from Maher had at last agreed to manage them. Finally, Andy Rourke returned to the Maher fold, replacing Dale on bass: both musicians turned up at Dione Studios in Chorlton to record demos of 'Handsome Devil' and the recently completed 'Miserable Lie', and Dale was informed by Maher that his services were no longer required. Soon afterwards the group were given the disappointing news that their work had been rejected by the moguls at EMI.

What is certain, of course, from practically every admirer's point of view and opinion, is that Morrissey *was* The Smiths – in their formative years often with Johnny Marr (as he had now started to call himself so as not to be confused with John Maher of The Buzzcocks) running a very close second; the two remaining members of the group regarded by many as not indispensable. Even Morrissey admitted, 'I think they were very lucky . . . I believe that if Andy Rourke and Mike Joyce had had another singer they would have gotten no further than Salford Shopping Centre.'

The Smiths crashed on to the Manchester pop scene, spreading rapidly across Northern England like a starburst, steadfastly refusing to be categorized, and establishing their importance with a series of statements, musical or verbal, inevitably controversial, which secured them a cult following, coupled with a love-hate relationship conjured up by the tabloid press, though Mike Joyce was quick off the mark to dispel this myth when he said, 'All that stuff about, Oh, The Smiths, you either love 'em or loathe 'em, is a load of bollocks. The mark that we made on music is more than what The Beatles did. I think it's more than what The Stones did.' Attractive they certainly were, but not over-glamorous like Culture Club or Adam and The Ants, and Morrissey and Marr, in spite of their later gimmicks and put-on campness, were not gender-benders. Lyrically, they were unique. For the first time in three decades British audiences were permitted to enjoy articulate verse set to equally rich, stylish music, and relating to a particular way of life. If British pop fans knew nothing about the *réaliste* songs on the Continent, where artistes had been wearing their hearts on their sleeves for three-quarters of a century, then The Smiths' repertoire pierced their imaginings like hot steel through flesh. In short, Morrissey and Marr's venture was original yet traditional, and in some respects intentionally uncommercial, proving that the time-honoured, 'old-fashioned' methods of regular airplay and concert appearances, as opposed to promotional videos, still held good and sold records. *Prince Charming*, the superb Adam and The Ants video with in-costume characterizations by the group and the actress Diana Dors, had appeared much better in celluloid than in sound only. Thus, The Smiths swore that they would never make videos, and by and large they kept their word.

On 6 January 1983, The Smiths played The Manhattan, once again with James Maker dancing, and with Morrissey showering the audience with handfuls of confetti which he pulled from his back pocket. Tony Wilson saw the performance, and it was anticipated that he might have been interested in negotiating a deal with Factory Records. Instead, he offered them an engagement at his Hacienda Club, early the next month. There they performed eight numbers – 'These Things Take Time', 'Jeane', and 'Hand in Glove' for the first time, and the second line of the latter, 'the sun shines out of our behind . . .', served as a 'warning' to would-be rivals that here was a force to be reckoned with.

At the Hacienda, flowers were incorporated into the Morrissey act for the first time – introduced, he said, to brighten the gloomy auditorium. Morrissey would have liked to adopt the lillium as his emblem – almost a *century* before, his hero Oscar Wilde had used these to decorate his rooms at Oxford. Instead, Morrissey opted for the more easily affordable daffodils or gladioli, depending on the season, but admitted when asked how much he had spent on flowers in the year following the Hacienda debut: 'I think it could have kept the DHSS afloat . . . they're virtually more important than the PA system.'

Shortly after the Hacienda show, John Muir of Babylon Books published 5,000 copies of Morrissey's second brief biography, *James Dean Is Not Dead*, and considered a third book – a compendium of lesser-known camp icons such as Terry Moore, Sandra Dee, Thelma Ritter and Agnes Moorehead, rounded off by an essay on the Queen of the Gallery-Girls herself, the outrageous Tallulah Bankhead. By this time, however, The Smiths' debut single was foremost in Morrissey's mind. 'Hand In Glove', coupled with a version of 'Handsome Devil', was recorded on stage at the Hacienda, financed by the group's manager, Joe Moss, and mixed/recorded at 10CC's Eric Stewart's Strawberry 2 Studio. The group, meanwhile, made their London debut on

23 March at the Rock Garden, and on 6 May they appeared in the same University of London bill as the outrageous Sisters of Mercy.

'Hand in Glove/Handsome Devil' was released on the Rough Trade label – whose best-selling acts at the time were Aztec Camera and Scritti Politti – a few days after the London show. Though it did reasonably well in the independent charts, clearly putting The Smiths on the music map, it did not make an immediate impression on the mainstream hit parade, though of course it has more than made up for it since. Not only the lyric contents of the songs raised a good many eyebrows. The sleeve depicted a 1950s rear-view shot of a naked young man (since identified to the author as gay porn-star Leo Ford, one-time lover of the outrageous diva, Divine) leaning languorously against a locker-room wall. (A limited number of these singles were released with discoloured sleeves – these have subsequently become collectors' items.) When asked by Catherine Miles of *Him* magazine if there was any significance attached to this at once suggestive and beautiful image, Morrissey's response was an honest one. 'I adore the picture. It evokes both sorrow and passion. It could be taken as a blunt, underhand statement against sexism, yet in using that picture I *am* being sexist. It's *time* the male body was exploited. Men need a better sense of their own bodies. Naked males should be splashed around the Co-op. I'm sure this would go a long way towards alleviating many problems, even that of rape.'

In the crowd at the University of London was John Walters, at that time producer for Radio One's famous *John Peel Show*. Walters was so impressed – especially when, after the show, he met Morrissey, who never answered a question directly, but preferred to prevaricate or philosophize – that he recorded four of their songs for the programme, which was broadcast on 31 May, and repeated by public demand five times in less than two years. Today, the recording is one of the most sought-after items in The Smiths' discography.

Three of the songs were already known, but the one which had the greatest impact was the superb 'Reel Around the Fountain'.

Though the lyrics to the song appear to be homoerotic, unless to tease and add to his essential mystique, this may not have been Morrissey's intention. In common with many interpreters of his genre he had adopted an asexual style in his work which in effect rendered his lyrics genderless. Adopting this characteristic some sixty years before, Al Jolson had crooned, 'I'm Just Wild about Harry', and no awkward questions had been asked then. This aside, Morrissey, with his predilection for certain types of British cinematography, had borrowed the phrase 'Take me and mount me like a butterfly' – spoken by lepidopterist Terence Stamp to Samantha Eggar in *The Collector* at a time when the word mount had a slightly different connotation, from the actual film-script; other lines from the song came from Shelagh Delany's *A Taste of Honey*, another favourite film. And when asked the question some years later, 'What is your idea of perfect happiness?' he would reply, tongue-in-cheek, 'Being Terence Stamp.'

The Peel session brought its rewards, too, for The Smiths were given a valuable spot on the equally eminent *David Jensen Show*, also on Radio One, though because of tabloid allegations of suggested paedophilia in the lyrics, 'Reel Around the Fountain' had to be dropped. The 25 August edition of the *Sun* ran a piece penned by Nick Ferrari which was headed, 'Child Sex-Song Puts Beeb in a Spin'. Other publications quickly followed suit. Ferrari had in fact confused the lyrics of 'Reel Around the Fountain' with those of 'Handsome Devil'. Morrissey attacked Ferrari for 'misinterpreting the facts', adding, 'What developed was a total travesty of the actual meaning of the song. Quite obviously we don't condone child molesting or anything that vaguely resembles it. What more can be said?'

Afterwards, The Smiths embarked on a seemingly endless

summer tour which included support slots at a miners' gala at Cannock Chase, Birmingham's Fighting Cocks, the Brixton Ace, a top-of-the-bill return to the Hacienda, and London's Lyceum and Dingwalls. And yet, in spite of the HOUSE FULL notices almost everywhere, the major record companies did not rush forth with lucrative offers, and in June 1983 Morrissey and Marr signed a fifty-fifty deal with Rough Trade, who did offer consolation in that they allowed their artistes a share of the profits of record sales. In fact, the money The Smiths earned for Rough Trade is thought to have saved the company from bankruptcy.

The Smiths were compensated by the BBC for being refused the airing of 'Reel Around The Fountain' by being offered a second appearance on *The John Peel Show*, and of course the hammering this song had been given by the tabloid hacks worked in their favour, even though the actual single of the song, coupled with 'Jeane', had been pressed and postponed. The new songs in the programme – 'This Night Has Opened My Eyes', 'Still Ill', 'Back to the Old House' – were years ahead of their time, and 'This Charming Man', with its striking 30-bar introduction by Johnny Marr, was chosen to be on the next single. It was released, with 'Jeane', in November 1983, produced by John Porter, who had previously worked with Steve Winwood and Ginger Baker. The cover depicted a scene from Cocteau's avant-garde film *Orphée*, with a mirror-embracing Jean Marais – Cocteau's long-term actor-lover who, when the photograph was taken in 1950, was regarded by cinema-goers as the 'most beautiful man in France'.

The Smiths performed the song on BBC1's *Top of the Pops* on 24 November 1983, on the eve of their return to the Hacienda. It brought them instant national acclaim, entered the charts, and peaked at number 25. Sadly, the group's success signalled the end of the road so far as Joe Moss was concerned – he left, not because of any particular dissension between himself and his protégés, but in order to spend more time with his family.

As for Morrissey – whilst he appreciated the fanatical following of The Smiths, which had virtually doubled overnight, and was in no way attempting to sound self-righteous – he is said to have remarked, 'People are dedicated to us because we deserve it. It's all quite natural because I really think we merit a great deal of attention.'

3

Hated for Loving

A performance by The Smiths at the Derby Assembly Rooms on 7 December 1983 was filmed, and two days later transmitted on BBC2's *The Old Grey Whistle Test*. There was some slight editing and the order of the songs had to be rearranged – the show had been cut short when fans had invaded the stage, not to mob Morrissey, but to hug him. These displays of affection set an important precedent which would continue into his solo career, and which would often be purposely misinterpreted by bouncers and security staff – frequently resulting in injuries, sometimes serious, to admirers whose only crime was to heed the Morrissey maxim 'I am human, and I want to be loved'. Even so, the songs themselves were untouched – the programme's producer actually insisted that 'Reel Around the Fountain' should be left in, in spite of possible media condemnation – and the programme acquired the group thousands of new admirers.

There was also consternation at this time when a dance-mix of 'This Charming Man' – even 'fabricated' versions of the same song, remixed on a 12-inch disc by the New York dance-producer, François Kervokian – was released apparently against the group's wishes, though it did bring them an invitation, engineered by the avant-garde American entrepreneur Ruth Polski, to play a New Year's Eve show at the New York Danceteria.

The Smiths' first trip to the United States, professionally and personally, was a disaster. Johnny Marr had temporarily split up with his girlfriend, Angie. Soon after arriving in New York, Mike Joyce succumbed to a bout of chicken-pox.

Morrissey stumbled during the performance, and fell off the stage. The group stayed at the Iroquois Hotel (next door to the famous Algonquin Hotel) on West 44th Street, where James Dean had resided for a while with his lover, Rogers Brackett, during his first visit to New York in 1951. Morrissey's night-time companions were a host of cockroaches and he could not get away quick enough. So, rather than accept a brief tour of the East Coast, the group unanimously opted to return to England – Marr to his flat in Earls Court and Morrissey to his new Kensington home, though not before the pair had summed up the American situation, and the way they felt, by writing 'Heaven Knows I'm Miserable Now'.

The Smiths' next single, 'What Difference Does it Make?/Back to the Old House', was released in January 1984, and reached number 12 in the hit-parade. There was a minor upset over the sleeve, which featured a still of Terence Stamp from the film *The Collector*, smiling radiantly and holding a glass of milk. The actor objected to this, and the sleeve was redesigned with an identical pose being provided by Morrissey himself. The original, like the misprinted first sleeve of 'Hand in Glove', quickly became a collector's item.

With three of their records occupying the top three positions in the independent charts, and having been voted Best New Act in the *New Musical Express* poll, The Smiths embarked on their first international tour, arranged by All Tour Booking, and kicking off at Sheffield University on 31 January. The tour manager was Phil Cowie, who entered the proceedings just as Oliver May, the group's road manager and a close friend of Johnny Marr's from his Altrincham days, was leaving. By the end of June, a period fraught with financial problems, illness and general unrest, they would have covered 51 dates, taking in lightning visits to France, Belgium, Germany, Holland and Scandinavia.

An unruly section of the audience almost ended The

Smiths' 3 March concert at Dundee University, when beer-
cans and water were thrown on to the stage. Morrissey
issued a stern ultimatum: 'Behave yourselves, or we leave!'
During several songs the more raucous fans respected his
wishes, but when they became rowdy again he left, returning
only when the management had restored order, and
announcing grimly, 'Dundee, the world is watching!'

During this year Morrissey began a brief but fruitful professional association with Sandie Shaw, the Dagenham-born
singer who had had her third British number 1 with 'Puppet
on a String' – the song with which she had won the
Eurovision Song Contest – when he had been just eight years
of age. Since this time Morrissey had casually worshipped
her from afar and their friendship was, like so many of
Morrissey's, the result of a lengthy correspondence. The title
of his 'Heaven Knows I'm Miserable Now' was based on
that of her late-sixties hit, 'Heaven Knows I'm Missing Him
Now', and she had responded by writing her own 'tribute'
which she had humorously entitled 'Steven, You Don't Eat
Meat'. Early in 1984 Morrissey offered her 'I Don't Owe
You Anything', one of the numbers performed by The
Smiths on *The David Jensen Show*, and 'Hand in Glove', the
group's first failed single. Sandie Shaw's recording of this
breezed into the charts, her first major hit in fifteen years,
and when The Smiths played at the Hammersmith Palais on
12 March she made an impromptu appearance and sang the
song with them. Two years later, Morrissey would duet with
her on her old hit, 'Girl Don't Come', and she pleased him
by covering two of his favourite songs – Lloyd Cole's 'Are
You Ready to be Heartbroken?' and Patti Smith's
'Frederick'. 'Working with her was like meeting oneself in a
former life,' Morrissey declared.

Sandie Shaw also covered The Smiths' 'Jeane', her finest
studio performance with the group and technically her greatest offering to popular music in more than a decade.
Whereas parts of her rendition of 'Hand in Glove' clearly

show some vocal strain, the other song is delivered with such simplistic intensity, perfect diction, and a backing vocal from Morrissey which serves as a voracious attack on the emotions, that a lump in the throat is almost inevitable. Neither did the fact that the narrator is addressing affection towards a woman deter the singer, who merely donned the Morrissey cap and interpreted the song without changing the gender. Explaining to Kris Kirk, a journalist from *Gay Times* greatly respected by the entertainment world, that she and another woman had once lived together as a means of combining their families for purely financial reasons between marriages, she stressed, 'It was a very real closeness. Sex wasn't involved at all but the relationship was really passionate, like that between Morrissey and Johnny Marr. There's no thought of sex in their relationship – just an absolute closeness between them in which they've found they best express themselves.'

One may not be certain, however, if Sandie Shaw lived up to all of Morrissey's expectations once he had met her in the flesh, so to speak, for a few years later he said, 'I don't hear from her. It wasn't exactly a friendship made in heaven . . . let's just put it that way without saying any more.'

On 21 April, The Smiths commenced what should have been an extensive European tour at the De Meervaart in Amsterdam, the next day moving on to the Brecon Festival in Belgium. One week later, at the Markthalle in Hamburg, they gave their longest performance to date, 25 songs; it was televised and the edited version shown on the programme *Rockplast*. Part of their show at the Eldorado on Paris was also screened – on the French showcase *Les Enfants du Rock*, and the magazine *Les Inrockuptibles* offered a free, subscribers-only CD featuring 'rare' live versions of the group's most famous songs, neatly housed in a cover depicting Teddy Boys in a provincial setting.

Foreign audiences were bemused to witness Morrissey gyrating about the stage with daffodils or tulips protruding from his back pockets, and on a number of occasions (in Britain, too, on *Top of the Pops*) with an entire bush! This, he claimed, was his way of demonstrating that the entire music industry was way over the top. Admitting that it was no more a particular statement than 'a silly schoolboy prank', he added with typical George Formby aplomb, 'People stop me in the street and say, "Where's your bush?", which is an embarrassing question at any time of the day . . . but I don't mind if people remember me for my bush, so long as it's for artistic reasons.'

One song which went down well in France was 'Pretty Girls Make Graves', with its suggestion of 'she's too rough and I'm too delicate' male-passiveness, long a favoured theme on the Continent.

Performing well, The Smiths obviously were, but they were no happier in Europe than they had been in New York – perhaps even less happy, for the strictly vegetarian Morrissey and Marr had to contend with the rigours of a fatty European diet. Thus, when the group were halfway through their tour and breaking off to fly back to London for an appearance on *Top of the Pops*, no one was surprised when Morrissey announced that they would not be returning – the dates in Zurich, Munich, Frankfurt, Cologne, Bremen and Vienna were unceremoniously cancelled.

The 25 April edition of *Top of the Pops* saw The Smiths in fine form, performing 'Hand in Glove' with Sandie Shaw, clad in black and with customary humour 'exchanging' traits – whilst the group appeared barefoot, the songstress writhed about the floor, emulating Morrissey's movements.

In the midst of this multi-faceted mêlée, on 20 February the group released *The Smiths*, their début album. Ten tracks had originally been recorded in former Teardrop Explode's lead guitarist Troy Tate's Elephant Studios, in a Wapping basement, during the summer of 1982, but Morrissey and Marr had deemed these unsatisfactory even though some time later most critics would agree that they were of a better sound quality than the ones on the subsequent album, which had been re-recorded, with additional material, by John Porter at Manchester's Pluto Studios over a period of just two weeks, and mixed at Eden Studios in London.

What is remarkable, and perhaps unique in the pop world, is the way in which these songs were written. Johnny Marr, in common with many modern musical virtuosi, preferred working in the studio, in direct contrast to Morrissey, who has always maintained that his happiest moments have been spent on stage – and it is perhaps significant that every singing legend, from Garland to Gigli, from Piaf to Pavarotti, invariably gave their best in front of a live audience. Morrissey also shared with some of the great singers the nerve-racking (for everyone, that is, but himself!) habit of last-minute arrivals, with the bonus of never disappointing. While Marr, Rourke and Joyce slaved away for hours, and sometimes days, perfecting the musical arrangements before presenting the tapes to Morrissey, he then either wrote the lyrics around them, or consulted his ever-ready source of notebook anecdotes and stanzas before turning up at the studio the next day to record his lyrics, as often as not with just one or two takes, over the music.

Three of the songs originally taped by Troy Tate – 'Handsome Devil', 'Accept Yourself' and 'These Things Take Time' – were replaced on the album by 'Pretty Girls Make Graves', 'Suffer Little Children', and Morrissey's purported championing of the dole queue, 'Still Ill', in which he questions the point of going to work when there are brighter sides to life.

This latter song is said to have been inspired by an event in the ever-traumatic life of Vivian Nicholson. 'Under the bridge we kissed / I ended up with sore lips' comes from *Spend! Spend! Spend!*, her ghost-written autobiography which was turned into a successful television film starring Susan Littler.

The Smiths reached number 2 in the album charts, for the

group sell-out venues and a wealth of en-route accolades. Once more, the sleeve became the subject of some controversy. It depicts a scene from Andy Warhol's underground film, *Flesh*, which had, perhaps ironically, been directed by Paul Morrissey, and which starred the in-house gay icon, Joe Dallesandro, who had once outraged American audiences by being interviewed naked on live television in a 'bubble-less' bath. Familiarly known as 'Little Joe' on account of his phenomenal endowment (inasmuch as 'Little John' had been thus named because he had been so very tall), the actor had played a rent-boy in the film, and the photograph depicted him semi-naked, perched on the bed next to his customer, who is licking his lips in anticipation of what is on offer. By the time the photograph reached the album sleeve, however, it had been heavily clipped and was in no way salacious – indeed, had it not been for the media reminding everyone *where* the photograph had come from, few people would have known that it had come from a soft-core porn movie at all.

The 'gay' issue was again explored/exploited, this time with some malice, a few weeks before the end of The Smiths' tour by a feature which appeared in *Rolling Stone*; to say that Morrissey was misquoted in it would not be putting it strongly enough. Morrissey had granted the interview during the afternoon preceding the group's show at the Hammersmith Palais. He spoke about pop music in general, and shared some of his literary inspirations with the journalist before turning his attention to British politics. Particular emphasis was placed on his opinion of the Prime Minister, Margaret Thatcher, of whom he concluded, mirroring the thoughts of many people living in North of England poverty-traps, 'She's only one person, and she can be destroyed. I pray there's a Sirhan Sirhan somewhere. It's the only remedy for this country at the moment.' When the feature came to be published, however, most of the emphasis veered towards Morrissey's alleged sexuality and the fact that he had admitted himself to be gay but celibate. This he had never done. Once again, the knives were out. Morrissey tried to laugh off the situation by stating that the 'gay' tag was but 'wishful thinking on the part of the journalist', though he was quite obviously hurt.

There were further press problems towards the end of May 1984 when the single of 'Heaven Knows I'm Miserable Now' was released – Morrissey appeared on *Top of the Pops* with protruding bush, oversized pink blouse, dangling crystal beads and checked jacket but none of these were as conspicuous as his unprecedented sporting of a hearing-aid. Some older Smiths fans, knowing Morrissey's love of nostalgia, assumed he was emulating the American fifties pop star, Johnnie Ray. The media suggested that he was mocking the afflicted. Neither explanation rang true. A deaf admirer had written to him, bewailing the misery and depression caused by her handicap, and, he explained, 'I thought it would be a nice gesture . . . to show the fan that deafness shouldn't be some sort of stigma that you try to hide.'

Nothing, however, caused The Smiths quite so much trouble as the flipside of the single, 'Suffer Little Children'. Although it had already received considerable airplay as an album track, when one of the murdered John Kilbride's relatives heard the song on a pub jukebox, he took exception and reported the matter to the *Manchester Evening News*. They printed a much overblown account which was picked up nationwide, and as a result both the single and album were withdrawn from sale by Boots, Woolworths, and several minor retail outlets. The problem was aggravated by the medias' and the retailers' inability or reluctance to read the small print on the record sleeve, which depicted Vivian Nicholson standing before a grimy suburban backdrop (the actor Frank Finlay had been the original choice, but he objected on the grounds that his image was 'inappropriate' for the promotion of a pop song). Seeing her with her sixties-style blonde hair and dated clothes, many of them assumed that Morrissey had, in an 'act of spite', used a photograph of Myra Hindley. Once again, this unfortunate young man became the victim of a smear campaign. A press release was organized, which included the lines: 'The song was written out of a profound emotion by Morrissey, a Mancunian who feels that the particularly horrendous crime it describes must be borne by the conscience of Manchester . . . it is a memorial to the children and all like them who have suffered such a fate.' Morrissey then wrote a heartfelt letter to Ann West, the mother of Lesley Ann Downey and for almost two decades the unofficial media spokeswoman/campaigner for the relatives of the other children murdered by Hindley and Brady. The pair met, became friends, and Morrissey and Marr donated a substantial portion of the 'offending' song's royalties to the NSPCC.

The Smiths' next single, 'William, it was Really Nothing' – the cover depicts Billie Whitelaw in *Charlie Bubbles* – entered the charts in 1984 with little fuss. Some sources suggested that it was Morrissey's homage to William Mackenzie, the singer from The Associates whom he met earlier in the year, and whom he described as 'like a whirlwind', though it is more likely that the lyrics owed much to the film *Billy Liar*, which tells the familiar story of the luckless lad who searches for escape from life in a humdrum town by daydreaming of the gold-paved streets of London.

Following the débâcle over their curtailed European tour, The Smiths had replaced Phil Cowie with a new tour manager, Stuart James, a former engineer/producer from Manchester's Piccadilly Radio who had several times worked with Ludus. Subsequently, Cowie threatened the group with legal action over money he claimed they still owed him, and Joe Moss, too, demanded payment for expenses he had incurred, notably on a public-address system; both matters were ultimately settled out of court. The Smiths now resumed their summer tour, with sell-out dates in Belfast, Dublin, Cork, a rained-off show on 2 June 1984 in Finland's Provinssi Festival, six shows in Scotland, and rounding off with the London 'Jobs For A Change' and Glastonbury Festivals. On a personal level, the group's engagement on 20 June at Blackpool Opera House was a bonus for Morrissey, who finally got to meet Vivian Nicholson – the pair were photographed strolling along the promenade.

Morrissey's passion for truth, honesty and freedom of speech was again put to the test on 12 October 1984 when, during the Conservative Party Conference in Brighton, an IRA bomb exploded inside the Grand Hotel, killing three people and badly injuring more than twenty more, including the wife of Norman Tebbit. Morrissey's statement 'The only sorrow of the Brighton bombing is that Thatcher escaped unscathed', a personal opinion which did not necessarily mean that he was in support of terrorism, was but one of many made by numerous entertainers, on television and radio programmes, and in working-men's clubs up and down the country. Because this was Morrissey, however, some journalists – whose own opinions may not have been too far removed from his own – decided to make an example of him by reminding readers of earlier comments which, in the light of the Brighton bombing, seemed more cruel. This, however, had no effect on a young man who was, after all, the representative of a large group of angry, disillusioned people, many of whom were dangerously close to the poverty line, if not already there. Thus, when asked in light of his earlier attack on the Prime Minister, what he would do if one of *his* fans shot her, he replied, 'Well, I'd obviously *marry* that person!'

What might have made matters worse, and what must have worried some of The Smiths' entourage, was that the group's second tour of Ireland – a ten-day stint which was scheduled to take in the Usher Hall in Belfast – actually kicked off on the day of the bombing. The main cause for concern, how-

ever, turned out to be everyone's state of health. The crossing was dire – Morrissey was one of the few not to suffer
from sea-sickness and Johnny Marr, who had the flu, became
so ill that he had to be rushed to hospital in Dublin, though
he was allowed to continue to his hotel after treatment.
There was also a repeat of the dietary problems which had
caused Morrissey and Marr to cut short their visit to Europe,
though the tour itself was a great success and the fans
behaved well.

After a lightning trip to France and a sell-out concert at
Versailles, The Smiths returned to England for a well-earned
rest, and Morrissey at once hit the headlines again by
expressing his views on Bob Geldof's virtually one-man
operation, Band Aid, the event which raised millions of
pounds for famine victims in Ethiopia, whilst of course
intentionally giving massive boosts to the careers of some of
the otherwise fading stars involved. On the face of it,
Morrissey's 'putting one's own house in order' priority statement – 'One can have a great concern for the people of
Ethiopia, but it's another thing to inflict daily torture on the
people of England' – made for sound common sense, as did
his later comment, 'People like Thatcher and the royals
could solve the Ethiopian situation within ten seconds, but
Band Aid was almost directly aimed at unemployed people'
– particularly when the starving country was itself dispensing millions on arms and was almost totally ignorant of birth
control. Most of the media, however, did not perceive things
from Morrissey's angle, and once again the young singer
found himself anathematized.

The Smiths' second album, *Meat is Murder*, was already
well under way, but to appease existing fans and hopefully
recruit new ones to their banner, in November 1984 Rough
Trade released *Hatful of Hollow*, a mid-price compilation
containing the songs from the Peel/Jensen sessions and other
rare numbers, housed in an attractive gatefold cover depicting the playwright Joe Orton. It was a rich and varied selec-

tion, covering every conceivable angst – from the self-con-
demnation of 'Accept Yourself' and the role-reversal of the
wealthy but unhappy schoolfriend of 'You've Got
Everything Now', to the ubiquitous story of the abandoned
baby in 'This Night Has Opened My Eyes'.

At the beginning of 1985, The Smiths' authority was challenged by three very different, gay-orientated groups –
Culture Club, Bronski Beat, and Frankie Goes To
Hollywood. Morrissey's frequently ambiguous lyrics, coming from a man who persistently proclaimed his celibacy, his
aversion to violence and his hatred of Margaret Thatcher
and the royals, his views on Band Aid and other such chari-
ties, coupled with his would-be violent approach towards
those opposed to animal rights – all these *causes célèbres* had
alienated him from certain sections of society, and endeared
him to many more. Now, he was to a certain extent threatened by the hard-sell tactics of these newcomers. Boy
George, with his feminine clothes, pancake make-up and
pigtails, crooned his way to the top of the charts with
'Karma Chameleon', and responded to the obvious questions regarding his sexuality with, 'I'd rather have a cup of
tea!' Jimmy Somerville of Bronski Beat, on the other hand,
offended moralists by giving in-depth interviews to the
tabloids wherein he discussed, in anatomical detail, every
aspect of gay sex. And Frankie Goes to Hollywood's raunchy
and sexually explicit 'Relax', when banned by the BBC,
zoomed straight to the top of the charts. The group would
have two more number 1s, equally controversial, before fading into obscurity as rapidly as they had ascended, prompt-
ing Morrissey's comment, 'Their career has been
orchestrated by unseen faces.' As for Johnny Marr, when
asked the pertinent question, 'What ailments and illnesses
can a Smiths' record cure?' he fought back (no doubt 'bor-
rowing' his response from his partner) with: 'It can ease the
paranoia of being celibate.'

Morrissey, an essentially moral man with a fondness for

titillation, yet with an astute knack of knowing exactly where to draw the line – allowing the listener to form his/her own opinion regarding the ambiguity of his lyrics and, as Sandie Shaw later said, to apply them as and when to his or her life situation – would never have considered competing with an outfit like Frankie Goes To Hollywood, so it was left to the moguls at Rough Trade to aim for that long-elusive top-spot. This they did by releasing not a smutty or suggestive song, but one with a catchy beat, lots of guitar riffs, and a sensible, dramatic lyric. 'How Soon is Now?', taken from the *Hatful of Hollow* compilation and backed with 'Well I Wonder', again utilized the theme of an intense, crippling loneliness, the consequence of a fruitless search for love.

'How Soon is Now?' only reached number 24 in the hit-parade, not because it was unchartworthy – indeed, many critics hail it as one of the best numbers The Smiths ever put together – but because the affordable price of the album had enabled just about every fan to own the song already. And in spite of the unprecedented success of the 'competitors', the readers of *New Musical Express* had just voted them Best Group.

The next two Smiths' singles, lyrically more intellectual than most of the stuff being churned out by their contemporaries, were less successful commercially than any singles Rough Trade had released since the original 'Hand in Glove'. 'Shakespeare's Sister', an ode to the lure of cliff-top suicide, and inspired by Virginia Woolf's essay *A Room of One's Own*, which she had addressed to the feminist element of Girton Ladies College – Morrissey once called it 'the song of my life' – reached number 26. 'That Joke isn't Funny Any More', which expressed the benefit of death inspired by solitude – in this instance, dying with a smile on one's face – barely scraped into the Top 50, and it is said that the group accused Geoff Travis, the promotions man at Rough Trade, of failing to secure their records the airplay being afforded their rivals. Their second album, however, more than made up for this discrepancy.

Meat is Murder, released in February 1985, went straight to the top of the album charts, and came at a time when there was a certain amount of ill-feeling within the group. Morrissey, having just been told of Andy Rourke's heroin addiction – a problem which had apparently been kept from him for some time, for the other members of the group had always been expected to maintain their frontman's very high moral standards – came dangerously close to firing him, but was persuaded not to do so by Johnny Marr, who gave his word that he would take care of his friend. This he did, enabling Rourke to control the habit for the time being. What is astonishing is that the story did not reach the press, something which would have presented Morrissey with a formidable dilemma.

The intended statement of *Meat is Murder* is that there is no ethical or justifiable difference between death in military action and the slaughter of animals for human consumption. It is, however, only a personal opinion, Morrissey stressed: 'I don't hate meat-eaters, but I've found that if I say to certain journalists that I'm a vegetarian, they immediately assume that I detest, to the point of death, anybody who eats meat. I get tired of this extremism ... if I say I hate royalty, it becomes scandalous. "Morrissey Has Planned To Drown Prince William!" Ha-ha! It's really ridiculous!'

The album sleeve was meant to prick the conscience, depicting a scene from Emile de Antonio's 1969 anti-Vietnam War film *In the Year of the Pig* – the inscription on the GI's helmet, 'Make Love Not War' was replaced with the album title, and Morrissey issued the statement, 'Violence towards animals is also linked to war ... where there's this absolute lack of sensitivity where life is concerned there will always be war.' Later, he attacked some animal rights groups for being too peaceable by adding, 'The only way we can get rid of the meat industry is by really giving people a taste of their own medicine.' When asked how he would greet

Colonel Saunders if he ever met him 'in heaven' he responded, after reminding his interviewer that it was very unlikely that the founder of the Kentucky Fried Chicken empire would ever *get* to heaven, 'I think I would resort to the old physical knee in the groin!' Some years later Morrissey would come very close towards taking legal action against the Norfolk turkey magnate, Bernard Matthews – the singer denounced him as 'the most despised person on earth' – for the use of a Smiths poster in a television advertising campaign without permission.

In order to hear the title track, placed at the very end of the album, the listener has the compelling task of ploughing through any number of crimes and emotions, mood, and changes of tempo, all of which naturally serve to make the overall work that much more potent. Crime, of course, has always provided a cherished though not necessarily obsessive Morrissey theme. 'I'm interested in the sense of celebrity, even on the level of murder,' he said later, 'and the fame attached to grisly crimes. I often wonder why people commit such crimes are treated like celebrities. It doesn't do the crime rate much good . . . everybody wants to leave their mark, nobody wants to be an ordinary, plodding citizen. And the lengths that some people will go to are quite enormous, for better or worse.'

Several of the songs from *Meat is Murder* warrant special mention. The music for 'Rusholme Ruffians', arguably amongst the best Johnny Marr ever wrote for The Smiths, was actually based on Elvis Presley's (Marie's the Name) His Latest Flame', and the famous Doc Pomus guitar riff recurs throughout – Marr's inspiration is said to have come from listening to the song at Wythenshawe Funfair, where he had once worked briefly on one of the rides. Morrissey's lyrics also centred around a fair – a very different, violence-orientated annual event which took place at Platt Fields, adjacent to the Manchester City football ground.

Another disturbing vignette is unfolded in 'I Want the One

I Can't Have', which graphically describes the murder of a policeman by a teenager. The skittishness of 'On the day that your mentality catches up with your biology!' is reminiscent of the later Morrissey utterance, 'Most people keep their brains between their legs!'. Then, there was his personal impression of Northern family life, 'Barbarism Begins at Home'. The supreme example of realism, however, has to be 'Meat is Murder' itself, for in this song The Smiths emulate in the most harrowing, disturbing manner imaginable the animals' route to their Calvary – the slaughterhouse. There are the moans of the cattle, the fierce proclamation that death for no reason is murder, and the sharpening and scraping of saws and knives, enough in fact to put some people off their carnivorous habits for life, which was of course Morrissey's intention. Whereas Andy Rourke converted to vegetarianism only temporarily – later claiming, 'Morrissey made you feel uncomfortable about meat in his presence – in the end you'd do it, but you wouldn't enjoy it' – Mike Joyce took the stance more seriously, saying, 'What stopped me from eating it were the lyrics to "Meat is Murder" ... I haven't eaten it since.'

The hastily put together, though excellent *Meat is Murder* tour opened on 27 February 1985 at the Golddiggers, Cheltenham. The group were played on to the stage with Prokofiev's 'March of the Capulets', from his *Romeo and Juliet* ballet suite, and it was blind adoration all the way. When fans – Morrissey called them his 'private and extraordinary club' – invaded the stage towards the end of the performance to embrace him, they were manhandled into the wings by bouncers, and roughly so, drawing forth so many complaints that The Smiths rectified matters by appointing more responsive security staff from amongst their entourage. There were 23 dates in all, complete sell-outs, with memorable concerts at the Brixton Academy, and the Royal Albert Hall on on 6 April where Morrissey duetted on 'Barbarism Begins at Home' with Pete Burns, the outrageous singer from the group Dead Or Alive – another frontman who had often fallen foul of the music press on account of his outspokenness. Morrissey said, 'I felt a great affinity with that situation. He's one of the holiest saints that ever walked the earth.' Later he joked with the press over their 'exchange' of birthday gifts: 'He sent me twenty-six roses . . . I sent him forty-eight naked sailors.'

In the middle of May The Smiths flew to Rome, where they had been booked for a concert at the Tendetrisce, and an appearance in a mediocre television show which had already been boycotted by several top European stars. The promoters, Virgin Italia, wooed the group as far as the rehearsal studio, but they did not do the show.

There were further problems in Spain when The Smiths, enraged with faults in the public-address system, cancelled a concert in San Sebastian. Hundreds of fans began chanting outside the concert hall, and windows were smashed when a scuffle broke out between fans and officials. The next stop on the road was the Paseo de Camoeons Festival in Madrid on 5 May, which was recorded and issued on an excellent bootleg album. Another bootleg doing the rounds at this time was *A Nice Bit of Meat* – and one is hard-put to make out if the title applies to the nude picture of Marilyn Monroe on the cover, or most fans' impression of The Smiths' singer? *A Nice Bit of Meat* included extracts from the group's early television shows, Johnny Marr's unique rendition of the Jimi Hendrix classic, 'Purple Haze', and the not often performed Morrissey credo, 'Unlovable'.

In Madrid, there was an allegedly heated argument between The Smiths and their manager, Scott Piering of Rough Trade, which heralded a parting of the ways, though some time later Piering did condone the unsinkable perfectionism which makes legends what they are by confessing, 'I just can't *help* but like him. On a professional level, he's a total nightmare. I don't think if he came to me on bended knees I would ever want to work with him again.'

Morrissey later defended The Smiths' tendency to change their management with alarming regularity by saying, 'I never found a manager who could deal with the whole situation without wanting creative input, without giving their opinions. They [managers] can't resist meddling, believing they too are making the new album, designing the cover. The Smiths was an absolutely closed society.'

4

The Boy With the Thorn in His Side

To bridge the gap created by Scott Piering's departure, Morrissey and Marr enlisted the qualified services of Matthew Sztumpf, the former manager of Madness, and it was he who put the finishing touches to The Smiths' forthcoming tour of the United States – a surprising package which would take them to Chicago, Detroit, Washington, Philadelphia, Los Angeles, and a roof-raising concert at the Kingswood Theatre in Toronto, Canada.

The first show in Chicago's prestigious Aragon Ballroom, on 7 June 1985, presented a problem when Morrissey – always full of surprises – demanded that a drag queen open the show, supported by a playback system. The hapless drag artiste was heckled from all sides and pelted with beer cans, and subsequently dropped a few days later. Neither was each leg of the tour made any the more pleasant for Morrissey because of his abject fear of flying, though he forced himself to cope with this, in view of The Smiths' increasing popularity. There was light relief, but no respite, from the group's hectic schedule when, on 20 June in San Francisco, Johnny Marr married his longtime sweetheart, Angela Brown ... and in an interview when for some reason President Reagan's name entered the conversation, Morrissey could not resist cracking, 'I'm sure they would have elected Joan Collins if she'd have been available!'

The American tour, particularly the open-air concerts in Los Angeles, was astonishingly successful, if far too short, though in truth The Smiths had never known quite what to expect. There had also been genuine outbursts of anger from

Morrissey over the decision made by Sire Records not to release single versions of 'William, it was Really Nothing' and 'Heaven Knows I'm Miserable Now' – an action which he had denounced as 'an absolute insult'. It is not known if the group had been invited to participate in Bob Geldof's most recent adventure – Live Aid, with simultaneous mass-audience concerts in Philadelphia and London, on 13 July, though bearing in mind what Morrissey had said about its forerunner, it is extremely doubtful they would have even considered the idea.

This time, it was Johnny Marr who raked up a minor controversy, not by condemning the actual event, but by expressing disapproval in a *Melody Maker* 'scoop' interview over two of Live Aid's stars. Fans of The Rolling Stones were shocked by his 'Keith Richard cannot play the guitar any more . . . I have no respect for him at all.' He also accused Bryan Ferry of trying to resurrect a flagging career by using the event to promote his latest single. A few days after the article, there were more media attacks against Morrissey when he 'shunned convention' by failing to turn up for *Wogan*, Terry Wogan's thrice-weekly chat show, an institution on BBC Television. On the 19 July edition, whilst the other three members of The Smiths were sweating it out in the London studio, Morrissey was quite comfortably at home in Manchester! Soon afterwards, in an interview for *Record Mirror*, he hit out at the lack of airplay The Smiths were getting, and no doubt worried the promoters at Rough Trade, by saying, 'I'm still too much acquainted with the whole aspect of poverty . . . I'm tired of being broke.'

Morrissey's concern was evident by the promotion of the group's next single, their first with a video. 'The Boy with the Thorn in His Side', again exploring the loneliness of the quest for love and with a cover featuring the sexually ambiguous American cult-writer, Truman Capote, peaked at number 23 in the charts.

On the flipside of the record is the prosaic 'Asleep', for

which Morrissey was accused of romanticizing suicide. In August 1985, he said, perhaps tongue-in-cheek, 'There are many people . . . who expect that I will be found dangling from some banisters, or swinging from the rafters in some darkened church,' which was in itself a gothically romantic notion.

On 22 September, The Smiths began a seven-date tour of Scotland, venturing to do a show at Lerwick, in the Shetlands. By now, the tension between the group and Rough Trade had almost reached saturation point. Their next album, *The Queen is Dead*, was practically complete and due for release at the end of the year – it was now put back, and the record company took out an interlocutory injunction to prevent them from signing with another label. In a moment's playfulness, and probably to relieve some of the tension he must have been feeling, Morrissey turned temporary journalist – in his capacity as unofficial spokesperson for Granadaland – and interviewed the actress Patricia Phoenix, one of the unsung heroines of the North after playing Elsie Tanner, the brassy tart-with-the-heart, in *Coronation Street*, and now sadly coming towards the end of her life. He called her 'simply a blizzard of professionalism', and added, 'You simply wanted to rush towards her bosom and remain there forever.' He also readily expressed his own personal opinion that *The Street* was now on the slide, particularly when faced with competition from the comparatively new Channel 4 soap, *Brookside*. 'The thing now is so empty – it's plotless. I thought Tracy Langton was probably the first real indication of the total erosion of the programme,' he said. 'There's some skill in *Brookside* – they actually make an effort. The script is not as relentlessly vaudeville as *Coronation Street*.'

A most extraordinary assignment was engineered at the end of the September. When asked by Channel 4's *The Word* to choose his own interviewer for a short profile on The Smiths, Morrissey – tongue-in-cheek, perhaps – selected

Margi Clarke, the garrulous Liverpudlian actress and self-proclaimed sex expert who had just scored a triumph in the film, *Letter to Brezhnev*. The rendezvous – 'somewhere in the Scottish Highlands, near some ruins' – was as controversial as the finished programme's content. The actress, whom Morrissey announced prosaically, though some might say spuriously, as 'a luminary, a Venus who rises from the waves', and addressed throughout as 'Margox', was told of his own ambition to act. This was arranged, of course, and a scene from *Letter to Brezhnev* was 're-enacted'.

Quite by mistake, Morrissey enters the ladies' toilet in a club, where Clarke and a friend are sharing a cubicle. Her own vocabulary when describing him leaves much to be desired as she espies him re-arranging his quiff in front of the mirror and yells, 'He's frigging gorgeous, like that bloke from *Doctor Zhivago*!' She then loans him her 'Choosy Cherry' lipsalve and the camera beats a hasty retreat to footage of The Smiths' show at the Glasgow Barrowlands!

On 31 January 1986, The Smiths appeared with Billy Bragg as part of the singer's Labour Party-inspired Red Wedge Tour – not an entirely rewarding experience, as Morrissey explained, 'Without wishing to sound pugnaciously poncified, I wasn't terribly impressed by the gesture. I can't really see anything especially useful in Neil Kinnock . . . but if one must vote, this is where I feel the black X must go.' On 8 February The Smiths joined forces with New Order and The Fall in a benefits concert at Liverpool's Royal Court Theatre – not for charity, but to aid the 49 local councillors, including Derek Hatton whom Morrissey declined to meet, who had rebelled against the government by refusing to set the legal rate.

Again, there were problems within the group, and not all of them financial. Andy Rourke's heroin problem had erupted again, and he was taking methadone substitute, an antidote which proved almost as disastrous as the actual drug when, during The Smiths' brief tour of Ireland, he played badly on stage. Morrissey was interviewed in Dublin by George Byrne, whose lengthy feature subsequently appeared under the banner headline, 'THE MANCHESTER MARTYR'. Byrne wrote in his introduction: 'The permutations and contradictions which Morrissey throws in the face of all who seek to analyse him would tax the mightiest machine IBM could produce.' There was nothing contradictory, however, regarding Morrissey's stance on drugs: 'I find heroin absolutely detestable, though a great many people who take it do so very willingly . . . and I think that the more the authoritarian finger is wagged at these people, the more inclined they are to suit themselves.' The recent anti-heroin campaign was also brought under close scrutiny. Morrissey branded it as 'little more than vote-searching', adding, 'I found it very absurd that the British government could care about people on heroin, when they could scarcely care about people who were killing themselves because of unemployment.'

Johnny Marr, in spite of his close friendship with Rourke, realized that radical but nevertheless humane measures would have to be taken and after careful consultation with Morrissey, the bassist was asked to leave the group with the proviso that he would be re-admitted to the fold should he kick his habit. The pair meanwhile auditioned and hired Craig Gannon, a friend of Marr's pal Simon Wolstoncroft who had played rhythm guitar for The Bluebells and Aztec Camera.

In the same interview with George Byrne, Morrissey discussed his recent attack on Margaret Thatcher quite openly, emphasizing that though he had meant every word, he felt that he had unnecessarily been taken to task for his comments because of the 'moronic' attitude of the music industry. He stressed, 'When people who are intelligent come along they want to get rid of them or gag them. So if these people want to maintain their jobs and whatever credibility they might have, they have to remove what they see as a threat by not playing their records. It's not because I'm a vile person, but because I have views.' He was equally outspoken when asked – bearing in mind his family background – for his reaction to the Anglo-Irish agreement: 'You can turn on the news and hear that six innocent people have been shot dead in Belfast, and it doesn't warrant comment, which I say with massive regret because death and murder are part of a situation which is obviously unbridgeable. I certainly don't think that in England there's any desire, politically, to make life any easier in Belfast. Distance gives great comfort to the politicians who have to deal with it.'

There was another no-nonsense, perfectly logical dig at Live Aid, for if the interviewer could ask for an opinion, then the interviewee certainly was not afraid of giving him his 'money's worth! 'The basic reason I found it troublesome,' explained Morrissey, 'was that it was accepted by the music industry because it confronted a problem that wasn't actually in our land. Distance made it remotely glamorous. I wonder, if Bob Geldof had been concerned with certain domestic problems would the idea have been so warmly embraced by the music industry? If we want to examine the Ethiopian problem we could almost say that if people stopped eating meat, then all the grain that went into the meat industry to force-feed animals could go to these countries. If people gave up meat, it would play a great part in the reduction of world starvation.'

In the song 'Stretch Out and Wait', Morrissey asks the would-be bearer of his progeny, 'Is there any point in ever having children?' In the near future he would tell a French reporter that this was the most personal song he had ever written for The Smiths because it centred around a very private experience. Now, when asked if he wanted to have children, he affirmed that though six youngsters were at times the norm, he would sometimes wake up and find the very idea revolting. 'Then the next month, I want to open an orphanage! I suppose until I do find someone with whom I would like to have masses and masses of children, the whole idea is just a grey blur. But it is odd to want to inflict children on this world ... though there are obviously some good things in the world, it is sometimes very difficult to find them.'

A few days after his dismissal, Andy Rourke was arrested for the possession of drugs and Morrissey, despite his aversion to such things, rushed to his aid. Soon afterwards, clean and well on his way towards getting cured, Rourke picked up where he had left off, though Gannon was retained – both appeared with The Smiths on a television show in the middle of May 1986 promoting their latest single, 'Bigmouth Strikes Again', taken from the forthcoming *The Queen is Dead* album and housed in a sleeve depicting a striking photograph of James Dean. The song was, of course, Morrissey's clever way of getting one over on his more condemnatory critics by reminding them, satirically, that he was not incapable of slapping himself in the face from time to time.

Listeners were slightly puzzled when, halfway into the song, a female voice started to harmonize with Morrissey's. Although sources stated at the time that her name was Ann Coats (this was a pun on Ancoates, a district of Manchester), it was in fact Morrissey himself, speeded up 'Pinkie and Perkie' fashion by a mischievous Johnny Marr! Again, because of lack of airplay, the record was not a great success, peaking at number 26 in the charts before plummeting.

Even The Smiths' severest critics could not disagree that *The Queen is Dead*, released in June 1986 and failing to top the album charts by a hair's breadth, was the proverbial cream of their crop. Some went one step further by nominating it Best Album of the Eighties. It certainly proved once and for all to all those 'non-believers' that Steven Patrick Morrissey was by far the most articulate songwriter of his generation. It contains an unprecedented diversity of emotions, crises and mood-swings. 'Frankly Mr Shankly', rich with flat Northern humour in the tradition of George Formby and Norman Evans, is based on the poetry-writing Mr Shadrack, the undertaker in *Billy Liar*, but amended slightly because Morrissey had had a teacher called Shankly. 'Cemetry Gates', sung over a jaunty melody, suggests that one actually can derive pleasure from mooching around cemeteries, whilst lamenting the loss of the talent which lies beneath the tombstones. 'Vicar in a Tutu' is a whimsical study of tabloid fascination in largely respectable people's private lives, a direct contrast to the cutting drama of 'There is a Light That Never Goes Out'. 'Some Girls are Bigger than Others', which refers to the Church Of The Holy Name, in Manchester's Oxford Road, is a funny song quoting *Antony and Cleopatra*, not à-la-Shakespeare, but directly from Amanda Barrie and Sid James in *Carry on Cleo* – and ending with Morrissey crooning a snatch from Johnny Tillotson's early sixties hit, 'Send Me the Pillow You Dream On'. 'Never Had No One Ever' tells of the dangers of the Manchester streets during the singer's first 'twenty years, seven months and twenty-seven days'. 'The Boy With the Thorn in His Side' has already been mentioned.

The most disturbing song on the album is the sombre, dirge-like 'I Know It's Over', Morrissey's personal credo in that in spite of, or maybe because of physical beauty, fame and intelligence, all that remains after one's quest for loving arms is an empty bed and a crippling loneliness, diminishing qualities which in themselves necessitate the reluctant continuance of life. Morrissey actually said at the time, never more serious, 'If I wasn't doing this, I don't honestly believe that I would want to live.'

Morrissey had been longing to attack the royal family again, in verse, ever since the success of 'Nowhere Fast'. (In August 1985, on the occasion of the Queen Mother's eighty-fifth birthday he had observed the crowds outside Clarence House on the television news, and had quipped, 'If the woman had died there would have been less, and I would have been hammering the nails in her coffin to make sure she stayed there!') What evolved, however, rather than a spiteful attack on Britain's best-loved grandmother was a tongue-in-cheek, gently anarchic attack on the Queen and Prince Charles. Britain, as seen through Morrissey's eyes and those of his disciples, was crumbling and on the verge of hopelessness and disaster. The balmy, good old days of the Empire were well and truly gone – as Morrissey said, 'We don't believe in leprechauns, so why should we believe in the Queen?' Reality, not pageantry, was thus urgently required to right the wrongs foisted upon the country by greed and tradition, and this longing to reclaim one's values could not have been better evoked than by Morrissey's decision to include a snatch from the First World War music-hall song 'Take Me Back to Dear Old Blighty', which had been resurrected in 1935 by Gracie Fields and Cicely Courtneidge, and performed by the latter to be featured in the film, *The L-Shaped Room*. This opened the number before running into the noisiest piece of Johnny Marr feedback imaginable. 'The Queen is Dead' is in every sense a unique *chanson grise*, in turns satiric, witty, biting but never gratuitously vicious, a one-act drama which would not have seemed out of place during the denouement scene of Shakespeare's *Richard III*, one of Morrissey's favourite historical characters, and one royal who had never been afraid of doing things 'off the mark'.

In the lyrics, making the highly unlikely comparison between himself and Prince Charles, Morrissey poses the question, 'Don't you ever crave to appear on the front of the *Daily Mail* dressed in your mother's bridal veil?' before remonstrating, having 'executed' the appropriate historical research, 'I'm the 18th pale descendant of some old queen or other.' And, having been inspired by Michael Fagin, who had recently broken into the Queen's Buckingham Palace bedroom and chatted to her casually while awaiting arrest, whilst envisaging 'her very Lowness with her head in a sling', he does not personally intend violence when coming face to face with his sovereign.

Then, skipping noisily through castration, law, poverty and 'the church who'll snatch your money', Morrissey becomes the relieved bearer of glad tidings when he announces, 'The Queen is dead, boys! You can trust me!' – before reverting to the usual Garboesque pronouncement: 'Life is very long, when you're lonely!' A masterpiece of timing, words and precision!

The French heart-throb actor Alain Delon graces the sleeve of *The Queen is Dead*, but there is also a photograph of The Smiths standing outside Salford Lads' Club, appropriately on the corner of a Coronation Street. Another picture was taken outside Albert Finney's old shop. Andy Rourke commented, 'It was a bit of nostalgia, a bit of Mancunian history, a bit of laddism.' Johnny Marr, regarding the title-track as one of the highlights of his life, said a few years later, 'When we listened back to it, it made the hair on the back of our necks stand up. It's what I'm most proud of with The Smiths and being involved with Morrissey, that juxtaposition of rock from a housing estate.'

While *The Queen is Dead* was 'irreverently' soaring high in the charts, The Smiths prepared for their second major tour of North America. Beginning in Ontario in July 1986 and ending in Tampa in September, their new tour manager, Sophie Ridley, had organized 24 dates in concert-halls, ballrooms and open-air theatres. A new single was released which, through lack of time, was promoted by video – in this instance, directed by the legendary Derek Jarman. 'Panic', backed with 'Vicar in a Tutu' (and Marr's stunning instrumental, 'The Draize Train' on the 12-inch) shot into the Top 10, providing the group with their biggest hit since 'Heaven Knows I'm Miserable Now'.

Morrissey's controversial lyrics for 'Panic' came about after the Chernobyl disaster of 26 April when, following the newsflash a Radio 1 disc jockey played Wham!'s 'I'm Your

Man'. The insensitivity of this gesture, coupled with Morrissey's loathing for the anti-Smiths disc jockey Steve Wright, precipitated the 'Hang the DJ' ending of the song, which was of course made all the more potent by Jarman's violence-inspired work.

The song was incorporated into Jarman's 15-minute film, *The Queen is Dead*, along with that number and *There is a Light That Never Goes Out*, a catalogue of disturbing images, homo-eroticism, the poetic morbidity of male beauty symbolized by a young man blowing smoke into a skull, the disturbing imagery of children innocently singing 'Hang the DJ!', and a semi-naked woman flying the Union Jack. Morrissey voted 'Panic' the best section of the film, confessing that he never actually met Jarman, who put the film together whilst The Smiths were in America – apparently, their only condition for allowing him to use their material in the first place.

The American tour was a tremendous success, even though (and in the light of Andy Rourke's recovery from his drug problem) the sheer pressure of the work pushed Johnny Marr into hitting the bottle – 'I just stopped liking the other members of the group, and I stopped liking myself,' he told the *New Musical Express* during the spring of 1991; however, homesickness was probably the reason for the sudden curtailment of their tour after the performance in Tampa, Florida, on 10 September, with the last four dates on Sophie Ridley's schedule being cancelled. What they did not know at the time was that they would never visit America again as an ensemble.

Prior to the 8 August concert in Cleveland, Ohio, Morrissey gave an interview with Frank Owen of *Melody Maker* which, through no fault of his own, caused him a great deal of pain when the article came to be published in Britain at the end of the month. To begin with, Owen's comments were gratuitously homophobic for no apparent reason other than to cause the singer acute embarrassment . . . in

what amounted to a researched walkabout of Manchester's
gay haunts, including pubs, clubs, and notorious 'cottaging'
spots such as the men's toilets in Whitworth Street, and casually referring to Morrissey as 'a big girl's shirt' the journalist
is alleged to have been threatened with a 'thumping' from
Johnny Marr, and even Danny Kelly, writing in the rival
New Musical Express a few weeks later, admitted that
Morrissey had been 'the victim of a lynch-mob'. Also, for
reasons known only to Owen himself, the article strongly
implied that 'Panic' smacked of racism, which is not the
case. Morrissey's complaint in the song – that much of the
music churned out by Radio 1 was, lyrically at least, inane –
was but a personal opinion, coming from an acknowledged
expert on pop and rock music, one whose comments as a
reviewer had once been welcomed by the music press. The
fact that he had since admitted to 'detesting' Stevie Wonder,
that Diana Ross was 'awful', and that he considered
Whitney Houston and Janet Jackson 'vile in the extreme' did
not mean that he was opposed to the colour of their skin,
nor did the later statement, referring to the heavy influx of
black music on *Top of the Pops*: 'I think something political
has happened and there has been a hefty pushing of all these
black artists and all this discofied nonsense into the Top 40.'
Others had criticized both his output and his persona, and
he had every right to criticize theirs and not be labelled a
racist.

In spite of the successes of 'Panic' and *The Queen is Dead*
– *Spin*, the American pop magazine, had voted the latter Best
Album Of All Time – Morrissey decided once and for all to
sever The Smiths' association with Rough Trade, and they
signed a lucrative contract with EMI, a move which brought
cries of 'treason' from some quarters, who accused them of
allowing the company to turn them into Britain's most
important group of the decade, only then to be dumped. In
fact, no one 'made' The Smiths other than the fusing of the
talents of Morrissey and Marr, who had in any case been

courted by numerous mainstream record companies since the end of 1983. For the time being, however, contractual obligations prevented them from signing with EMI, and in November 1986 Rough Trade issued the single 'Ask', coupled with 'Cemetry Gates'. The A-side took a cynical peek at adolescent solitude, in this instance an evocation of Morrissey's pen-pal youth wherein the sacrificial narrator spends 'warm summer days writing frightening verse to a buck-toothed girl in Luxembourg' ... though with Morrissey there is an essential reminder that we are living in a real world: if love fails to bring the couple together, then the bomb certainly will!

The 12-inch/CD versions of the record featured The Smiths' very unusual cover of the Twinkle song, 'Golden Lights', without doubt the most harmonious number they ever performed. It had been penned by Twinkle during the sixties as an ode of despondency to her lover Dec Cluskey, the singer with The Bachelors. As with Sandie Shaw, Morrissey had been writing to her for some time – impressed by a newspaper feature revealing her fondness for animals. 'I think he's wonderful,' Twinkle said in a recent interview. 'I've never met him, and I know he has a strange reputation ... but he must be very kind underneath because he too loves animals. I'm very grateful to him for all that he's done.'

Another friendship which came as the result of letter-writing was Morrissey's close association with Kirsty MacColl, who was asked to provide backing vocals for 'Ask' and 'Golden Lights'. The talented daughter of Ewan MacColl told me, 'I was working New York. My manager called and said he'd found a letter from Morrissey on my doormat. All it said was, "Sing with me!" I didn't know what to make of it, so I went down to Rack Studios, and met Johnny Marr and his wife. Johnny said, "Moz is in there. Go in and sing with him!" I was terrified, but I did it. Morrissey greeted me as though he'd known me for years. He's one of the nicest, kindest men I've ever met.'

Imagery was potent during The Smiths' provincial tour, which began at the Carlisle Sands Centre on 13 October 1986. Most evenings, Morrissey courted controversy by parading a banner inscribed THE QUEEN IS DEAD. During 'Panic' he sported a Steve Wright T-shirt . . . and dangled a noose! Such provocation, alas, attracted a new kind of spectator to The Smiths' camp – thugs, who attended their concerts solely to spit, heckle, and make nuisances of themselves. At Newport on 19 October, the group were halfway through their act – Johnny Marr had just played 'The Draize Train' – when Morrissey leaned forward to shake a fan's hand and was dragged head-first off the stage. He banged his head on the floor and was taken to hospital with suspected concussion, though thankfully his injuries were only superficial. One week later, during the first song at Preston Guildhall, he was hit in the face by a projectile. This time the concert was abandoned, resulting in a riot and several arrests.

Craig Gannon, the 'Fifth Smith', left the group towards the end of the tour – it is said forcibly, and with no small amount of ill-feeling. The guitarist alleged that he had been underpaid during their last American tour, and that Morrissey and Marr owed him co-writing royalties for 'Ask'. Several years later, Gannon would be adjudged a not inconsiderable sum after taking the matter to the high court.

The Smiths, meanwhile, were engaged to top the bill in an Artists Against Apartheid gala at the Royal Albert Hall on 14 November, supported by their fellow Rough Trade 'deserters', The Fall, proving by and large that the really important showbusiness moguls had completely ignored the racist slurs. The show had to be cancelled when Marr, heavily under the influence of drink, and driving without a licence, crashed his BMW in the pouring rain near his Bowden home. Though the car was a virtual write-off, most of Marr's injuries were caused by his falling down several times while stumbling away from the scene of the accident in a shocked state – there was some damage to his hands, and he suffered whiplash which meant he had to wear a neck-brace, though when the show went ahead at the Brixton Academy on 12 December, he was in sparkling form. Neither would anyone have argued the irony of Morrissey's lyrics to 'There is a Light That Never Goes Out', in view of the accident.

The unruly element had been removed from Smiths spectators and the fans at the Brixton Academy were well-behaved; indeed the filmed footage of the event pays testimony to how much love Morrissey could extract from these people. Fifty young men, most with tears in their eyes, crushed up against the barrier to chant along to the words of 'There Is a Light That Never Goes Out'. One fan later told me, quite seriously, 'I thought about ancient Rome – you know, when the Emperor used to walk through the streets, and point at someone and say, "Citizen, fall on thy sword!" Most of those apostles out there were so crazy with admiration for Morrissey he could have asked them to do anything.'

What the audience did not know was that they were watching their idols' very last British performance. Conflicting pressures placed on the slender shoulders of Johnny Marr, some self-inflicted, coupled with Morrissey's mercurial character and mania for nothing less than perfection – elements which had contributed to his already being hailed as a living legend, at just twenty-seven – had pushed the partnership towards the point of no return.

In an exclusive interview with the French magazine *Les Inrockuptibles*, setting a trend which would reveal him as more direct, receptive and relaxed with foreign journalists than with British ones – by and large because they printed his observations verbatim, without adding prejudiced comments and improvisations of their own – Morrissey told Mishka Assaya, 'I'm afraid the day's going to come when I'll have to bid farewell to the past. It hasn't come yet, but it will. It seems inevitable that we will split up one day because there's only so much in each of us to give. When it becomes hard for me to concentrate or write songs . . . when it no longer seems that I'm doing the right thing, I'll stop.'

The Smiths' next single, 'Shoplifters of the World Unite' – title courtesy of a Manchester socialist rag, cover courtesy of Elvis Presley, and the line, 'My only weakness is . . . well, never mind!' purloined from a 1952 television drama featuring James Dean – also bears an anarchic ring, with the narrator's attempts to dwell in a real world thwarted by the fact that he is bored before it even begins. It reached number 12 in the charts. Just as compelling is the flipside, 'Half a Person', which tells of a six-year search for one's idol, necessitating a trip to London where, if one has five seconds to spare, one may hear the story of the singer's life . . . humdrum as Billy Liar's, maybe, but not lacking in wit, as the narrator books himself into the YWCA, asking meekly, 'Do you have a vacancy for a back-scrubber?'

During the spring of 1987, The Smiths were in the middle of recording *Strangeways Here We Come*, their penultimate album for Rough Trade, who in the meantime released the mid-price compilation, *The World Won't Listen*, containing many of their most celebrated songs, and the previously unreleased 'You Just Haven't Earned It Yet, Baby', a number very reminiscent in parts of Marianne Faithfull's 'Is This What I Get For Loving You, Baby?'. The album reached number 2 in the charts, at around the time Sire, The Smiths' American record company, released *their* compilation, the aptly titled *Louder Than Bombs*, which was much more expensive but still good value as it contained twenty-four songs. Complaints from record buyers, however, precipitated Rough Trade into releasing a cheaper edition, which barely made the Top 40.

On 7 February, the group flew to Italy where they participated in the San Remo Festival, on a revolving stage, sharing some of the accolades with Spandau Ballet and The Pet Shop

Boys. There was a new manager, Ken Friedman, a 29-year-old go-getting American who had organized Simple Minds' recent tour of the United States and UB40's headlining trip to Russia. Friedman's aspirations, that The Smiths should be universally massive, playing to 50,000-plus stadia, was frowned upon by Morrissey, who at once recognized the new manager's inability to understand not just him, but The Smiths' culture. Dissension therefore led to an inevitable clash of personalities, the first between Friedman and Pat Bellis, the group's press-officer who subsequently resigned. There were further problems when Morrissey failed to turn up for one of Friedman's video shoots.

At around this time, the single, 'Sheila Take a Bow', said to have been written in honour of Shelagh Delaney, the creator of *A Taste of Honey*, was released, housed in a cover depicting the Andy Warhol starlet, Candy Darling. It is a catchy song, its title name perhaps deliberately misspelt by Morrissey, who added a teasing touch of gender-bending with the lines 'You're a girl and I'm a boy . . . I'm a girl and you're a boy', and camp advice in the way of, 'Boot the grime of this world in the crotch, dear!' Shelagh Delaney's photograph had appeared on the cover of *Louder Than Bombs*. As for Candy Darling, perhaps the most outrageous transsexual to hit America during the late sixties – and like all the Warhol protégés, with the exception of Joe Dallesandro, to end up dead of a drugs overdose – was proclaimed the number one heroine in Morrissey's 'Camp Hall of Fame'; as he later admitted, 'To be able to inflict Candy Darling on the record-buying public was a perfect example of my very dangerous sense of humour!' 'Sheila Take a Bow' reached number 13 in the hit-parade.

Strangeways, Here We Come was recorded during the spring of 1987 at the Wool Hall, Bath – an apparently relaxed sojourn of sorts which bowed to not unprecedented pressure once the album had been completed. Johnny Marr told Morrissey that he was thinking of terminating their partnership, though he did claim at the time that the singer was his best friend. Morrissey and the other two members of the group were stunned, and insisted that they should all stick together, especially as they were about to begin record-ing with EMI; and that same week they had also contracted to film a *South Bank Show* documentary charting their suc-cess, one of the few occasions that a pop group had been awarded such an honour.

For the time being, therefore, the split was postponed. Marr announced that he was going to take an extended hol-iday, suggesting that everyone else should do the same, and it was assumed that upon his return the group would take up where it had left off. They had already decided that their next single, their last for Rough Trade, should be 'Girlfriend in a Coma', an unusual choice, perhaps, considering how much material there was in the can, and it was Morrissey who suggested recording two new songs for the B-side. The session took place in late May at Grant Showbiz's home stu-dio in Streatham, an episode which was later described by Johnny Marr as 'utter misery'. 'Work is a Four-Letter Word', from the film of the same name, had first been recorded by Cilla Black during the sixties. As for 'I Keep Mine Hidden', Morrissey reflected, 'When I play Smiths' records, which I do a lot, that song is always the first I play. And it's the one that makes me feel the happiest.'

Soon after the Streatham session, Johnny Marr flew to Los Angeles, and whilst there met up with Keith Richard, whom he had attacked in the press not so long before. He called it 'an enlightening experience', and Richard allegedly told him, 'The music business isn't worth knocking yourself out for. It's not worth killing yourself or stepping on other people.' Marr, it would appear, heeded the advice, very much to the chagrin of The Smiths and their fans.

Over the next few weeks, the music press abounded with conflicting stories concerning the group's 'demise'. An article appeared in the *New Musical Express* under the banner headline, SMITHS TO SPLIT, though thus far it was little more than speculation. The piece maintained that Morrissey and Marr were not on speaking terms, and had not been for several months. This brought the waspish threat from the Morrissey camp: 'Whoever says The Smiths have split shall be severely spanked with a wet plimsoll.' Marr actually accused his partner of engineering the article in order to expedite the end of the group, but as the singer had persistently denied any signs of a break-up, taking into account his unswerving honesty in the past, this would seem extremely unlikely. Iestin George of the *New Musical Express* told me, 'Obviously, we did have one or two leads which came from neither Morrissey nor Marr, but by and large we were just spot-on with our guesswork.'

Some time later, Johnny Marr changed his tune and confessed to Dave Haslam of the *New Musical Express*: 'It was a hideous private explosion, and also a hideous public explosion turned into a soap opera by the papers. Nothing that was said was true. People around us, both on my side and Morrissey's, handled the whole thing so badly that it became their whole trip. It had nothing to do with how I feel about Morrissey and how he feels about me. I despise the way we became public property.'

The latter comment, of course, could quite easily have been misinterpreted by Smiths' fans as one of ingratitude, for the group had been made and nurtured by the public for the last five and a half years, a public which was now bereft. The split proved too much for one young fanatic in Denver, Colorado, who went to his local radio station and detained a disc jockey at gunpoint until he had held a suitable 'wake' – four hours of non-stop Smiths records. 'It was worth every minute I'm going to spend in jail,' he sobbed as the police handcuffed him and led him away.

The Smiths' passing was lamented by the profession, too. Billy Bragg, who had criticized Morrissey and Marr for having agreed to record with EMI in the first place said, 'It's going to be a poorer world without them.' Marc Almond accurately forecast the future: 'Splitting The Smiths at their peak will ensure that their aura stays intact. Without doubt, Morrissey will go on to greater heights.' An anonymous commentator wrote with typically Morrisseyian humour:

> Turned out finally that Morrissey and Marr weren't the soulbrothers, the creative peas in a pod we'd imagined, but more like Dennis the Menace and Walter, with Dennis fed up of wearing the tutu and bunking out, freelance, with various hoary old rock institutions.

Some of the so-called 'rock institutions' with whom Marr had worked were Quando Quango, and Everything But The Girl (1984), Impossible Dreamers (1985), and Billy Bragg himself (1986) – all as a part of his extra-Smiths curriculum, and accepted by them. His more recent work with Bryan Ferry, however (in spite of his former severe criticism of Ferry, Marr had appeared with him in Los Angeles on *Saturday Night Live*) and his guesting on Talking Heads' *Naked* album, scotched the rumours that The Smiths might have been getting together again, and finally on 8 August the guitarist dropped his bombshell. 'I've already recorded some stuff and it's gone well – there's every chance I'll be forming a permanent group. I definitely want to have some live dates set up by the New Year at the latest,' he announced in the *New Musical Express*.

The absolute truth concerning The Smiths' demise, however, came from Morrissey himself, who blamed it on immaturity, bad handling . . . and the *New Musical Express*.

Nothing would have happened if the *NME* hadn't listened to certain rumours concerning Johnny's intentions. That paper is largely responsible for The Smiths' split. I was furious with them. They brought out the coffin long before the corpse was cold. Their attitude traumatized me.

They printed so many lies about us – so much so that the rumour became a reality. If everyone had kept their mouths shut, our problems would have been resolved, in private.

5

I Would Sooner Be Just Blindly Loved . . .

Having been reluctantly but ultimately convinced that The Smiths would never play together again – Johnny Marr had firmly ruled out any farewell appearances – Morrissey engaged Stephen Street as his producer/songwriting partner, and by mid-September 1987 after Morrissey's official announcement regarding The Smiths' demise, the pair had already begun work on his forthcoming debut album as a solo artiste.

Street had first brushed shoulders with Morrissey and Marr during the recording of 'Heaven Knows I'm Miserable Now', and he had produced The Smiths' final album, *Strangeways, Here We Come*, which Rough Trade released on 28 September. Morrissey was of the opinion that it was the best album the group had ever done, and when asked why he had chosen that title, responded, 'Because the way things are going, I wouldn't be surprised if I was in prison twelve months from now.' Then he added mischievously: 'I don't have any particular crimes in mind, but it's so easy to be a criminal nowadays, I wouldn't have to look far!'

More in the realist tradition than anything the group had ever done before – its emotions range from the cloaked bitterness of 'Unhappy Birthday' to the romanticized bedside dramatics of 'Girlfriend in a Coma', from the abject indifference of 'Death of a Disco Dancer' to the surrealist tale of Troubled Joe, the mysterious narrator of 'A Rush and a Push and the Land is Ours' – the album formed the perfect swansong for the partnership hailed by one critic as 'The Lennon

& McCartney of the Eighties'. Of the ten songs, 'Stop Me if You've Heard this One Before' was chosen as the group's next single release, but had to be aborted after the BBC complained over the lines, 'The pain was enough to make / A shy, bald Buddhist reflect / And plan a mass murder.' Only recently, a man named Michael Ryan had gone crazy and shot dead seventeen people in a provincial town, before turning the gun on himself, and the song – though recorded some months before this tragic event – was branded 'tasteless', and never once graced the airwaves. This, not unexpectedly, brought the acid comment from Morrissey: 'They said people would instantly have linked it to Hungerford and it would have caused thousands of shoppers to go out and buy machine-guns and murder their grandparents.' Geoff Travis of Rough Trade therefore opted for 'I Started Something I Couldn't Finish', a beautiful, romantic song about an illicit love, for which Morrissey had dipped his pen into Wildean ink and even purloined some of the great scribe's unnecessary suffering.

This, and the very last Smiths single released during their lifetime – the haunting 'Last Night I Dreamt that Somebody Loved Me' had an introduction, courtesy of the BBC sound-effects library, comprising crowd noise recorded at the time of the miners' strike – both reached the Top 30, and might have fared better had the group stayed together long enough to complete their promotion.

Arguably the most unusual song on the album, and therefore one of the most fascinating, is 'Paint a Vulgar Picture', yet another phrase borrowed from Oscar Wilde, and one which enabled Morrissey to hit out at the 'death-means-profit' element of the record industry. A famous singer has just died, and while one fan mourns, the 'sycophantic slags' at a record company meeting, who in all probability could not stand him when he was alive, are now content to regard him as a worthwhile investment by making the decision to repackage and re-release his records. From Morrissey's point of view, death makes his hero completely untouchable. There were, of course, inevitable comparisons to be made in such a situation with the recently deceased Smiths, though a few months later, Morrissey put paid to the rumour by cracking, albeit seriously, 'If another compilation appeared, I think people would stone Geoff Travis to death.'

The lamented star was, in fact, Billy Fury, of whom Morrissey had said, 'He's virtually the same as James Dean. He was entirely doomed too, and I find that quite affectionate.'

Strangeways, Here We Come invited plaudits galore from the music press, some of whom had already reported an alleged large number of suicide attempts, and a few successful ones, amongst bereaved fans who, with only memories of their favourite group to assuage their bedsit depression, had refused to compromise and look towards the future. Morrissey hit out at such reports, claiming that anyone with suicidal tendencies must have already had them *before* The Smiths appeared on the scene. *Smash Hits* wrote, eulogistically but sensibly:

> Rarely have a group inspired such blind devotion, or sheer hatred, as The Smiths: people either dissolve into a quivering, adoring heap on hearing Morrissey's mournful tones, or hurl the nearest hard object at the record player. So what is there to say? Only that The Smiths were one of the few bands who got better as time went by, and if you fail to be moved by songs like 'Last Night I Dreamt Somebody Loved Me', then you're missing out on a beautiful experience.

The South Bank Show was broadcast by Independent Television on 17 October 1987, and on the eve of this Morrissey told one journalist, 'The Top 40 has never been as abysmal as it is now – anything that reflects life as it's lived doesn't really have a place any more.' The unexpected dissolution of the Morrissey-Marr alliance had necessitated a last-minute rewrite of Tony Knox's film, which turned out to be good, though not definitive. Indeed, some authorities dismissed it as disappointing. It begins with archive footage of George Formby plucking his ukulele and toothily singing 'Why Don't Women Like Me?', cleverly running into 'This Charming Man'. Music journalist Nick Kent, looking emaciated, appeared and called The Smiths 'the first original English pop-group', bravely proclaiming that a decade hence they would be held in the same esteem as The Beatles were then. Morrissey prevaricates, as only he can with On stage I'm the normal me . . . or the *abnormal* me, perhaps.' Johnny Marr reflects, 'Arrogance was our forte.' Sandie Shaw, shown performing 'Hand in Glove' on *Top of the Pops*, says, 'He hides behind other people's experiences' – proof of Morrissey's devotion is then revealed by the photograph of him kneeling at her feet clutching a rosary. Vivian Nicholson is also seen, along with Andy Rourke and Mike Joyce, and the film closes with Morrissey's prosaic interpretation of the future as he proclaims, 'I think this is more or less the end of the story. Ultimately, popular music will end. The ashes are already about us, if we could but notice them.'

For the singer, the winter of 1987–8 was an apprehensive period. On a professional level he had worked closely only with Johnny Marr, and such a powerful presence must have been agonizing to cope without – not just as a musician and arranger, but as a friend and guiding hand. In fact, he and Marr had not been in touch with each other since the previous May. Stephen Street prescribed the perfect anodyne by engaging Vini Reilly, the guitarist with Durutti Column, whom Morrissey knew very well and, more important, trusted. There were the inevitable teething troubles, brought about by Reilly's coming to terms with the singer's still unorthodox method of writing and constructing a song around a particular piece of music, and his own, perhaps subconscious, tendency to compare himself with Johnny

Marr, whose aggressive riffs had occasionally compelled Morrissey to strain towards the upper register at a time when his vocal powers had not been fully developed. In fact, Reilly's gentle but effective style was better suited to bringing out the melody and passion in Morrissey's voice, with the more dramatic moments intensified by Andrew Paresi's fine work on the drums.

One of the songs worked on at the Wool Hall Studios in Bath was 'Suedehead', which EMI released as a single in February 1988, coupled with 'I Know Very Well How I Got My Name', a song which owes its title to an embarrassing incident in Morrissey's youth when, infatuated with David Bowie's 'Starman' period, an attempt to dye his hair yellow had backfired, leaving him with purple tresses! The record shot to number 5 in the charts, peaking higher than any previous Smiths single, and offering Morrissey exactly the boost he needed at this the most critical stage of his career.

'Suedehead' owes its title to the 1971 novel of the same name by Richard Allen, one of a series recounting the often violent adventures of a group of racist, anti-gay skinheads with overgrown hair. Sequels to the original book, which many adolescents kept hidden under their mattresses along with girlie magazines and other teenage paraphernalia, include *Dragonskins* and *Mods Rule*. Morrissey himself described 'suedeheads' as '. . . outgrown only in the hair sense, not meant to be football hooligans, so obviously much less interesting'. He then eradicated confusion by confessing that the song has nothing to do with skinheads at all – he had chosen the title quite simply because the word had appealed to him.

As with many Morrissey songs, this one ends in irony. The 'intruder' who has invaded the singer's privacy, no doubt to unearth a few secrets, draws from him the concluding, almost shoulder-shrugging line, 'Still, it was a good lay.' When asked if there had actually been 'a good lay', whilst admitting that the song *was* about someone in particular,

Morrissey quipped, 'No. I just thought it might amuse someone living in Hartlepool!'

Nothing to do with skinheads either is the superb promotional film for 'Suedehead'. Back in 1985, Morrissey had said, 'I would like to go to Indiana and mess with James Dean's soil, but so many others have done it. They've taken away the monument and the grass. What's left for me?' Produced by his close friend Tim Broad, who had directed The Smiths' 'Girlfriend in a Coma' and 'I Started Something I Couldn't Finish', and with a guest-appearance by Morrissey's nephew, the film presents a rich, thoughtful and ultimately rewarding tapestry of Dean images, centering on Morrissey's visit to Fairmount, the town of the actor's birth: the singer in his bath with typewriter, photograph of Dean and a volume of Byron (Byron was Dean's second name), one of his letters, the edition of *Fairmount News* containing the announcement of his death, a poster of Richard Davalos (the actor from *East of Eden* who had appeared on the cover of *Strangeways, Here We Come*), and a bathmat – at that time one of Morrissey's most prized possessions, a gift from an American fan – inscribed THERE IS A LIGHT THAT NEVER GOES OUT. Morrissey is also shown strolling through the snowbound streets of Fairmount, pausing to read from Antoine de Saint-Exupéry's *Le Petit Prince* (Dean's favourite book), posing on Dean's 1940s motorcycle, driving Dean's uncle Marcus Winslow's tractor on Dean's farm, studying his hand and footprints indented in cement in the barn when he was just twelve and aspiring towards the Lee Strasberg school of method-acting, playing his bongo-drums. The film ends at the graveside, with Dean's image superimposed – one legend surveying another surveying him.

For many, the brief *Suedehead* film was regarded as a turning-point for Morrissey, whose own 'acting career' had only recently begun and ended with four lines in Phil Redman's *Brookside* spin-off *South*, which was shown on Channel 4. Strangely, the film – which had been vetted and approved by

Marcus and Ortense Winslow – invited criticism from the tabloids, particularly a severe exclusive from the *Daily Mirror* headed WEIRD: MORRISSEY SITS ON JAMES DEAN'S GRAVE! This in itself was misinterpretation, and when its reporter, Gill Pringle, stated that the singer had 'wept at the graveside', she was challenged by Tim Broad, who added, 'Morrissey is a genius and a poet . . . and a die-hard fan. In some ways I think Dean is his spirit guide.' Morrissey hit out with a scathing, 'Gill Pringle will only commit to paper anything that isn't true. Having no real access to artists she consequently creates fictional quotes to disturb the millions of readers who automatically overlook her page.'

Morrissey's debut album, *Viva Hate* – which he described as 'a lofty piece' – was released in March 1988, and took no time at all to reach the top of the album charts. Asked why *Viva Hate*, when he exuded and imbibed such obvious devotion, he answered reprovingly, 'I find hate omnipresent and love very difficult to find. Hate makes the world go round.' When asked if he blamed anyone or anything for his being alive, his response was no less philosophical, 'I don't blame anyone for bringing me into the world, but I do feel that life is excessively overrated.' His dissatisfaction with himself and his self-confessed ugliness – the latter aspect refuted by every single one of his fans – were also brought to the fore at a press conference at London's Hyde Park Hotel, at which he avowed: 'I often pass a mirror, and when I glance into it slightly I don't recognize myself at all. You look into a mirror and wonder, "Where have I seen that person before?" Then you remember – it was at a neighbour's funeral, and it was the corpse.'

Viva Hate contains twelve songs, and Stephen Street, able to admit to the *New Musical Express* now that The Smiths were no more that he had not liked many of their songs, continued, 'It's only since I've heard this new material that I've realized how major a talent he is. Where it's sad and emotional, it's really heartbreaking stuff. It's far better than anything The Smiths ever did.' Alan Jackson wrote in the same publication:

> By proving he can work successfully with Stephen Street he is delivering a slap in the face with a wet fish to the nudging ranks of non-believers who felt he would fall apart without the support and strange haircut of Johnny Marr ... *Viva Hate* finds Narcissus poking a stick into the murky waters of his private pond, disturbing and distorting his reflection and seeming not to care if it detracts from his appearance. It's a brave record, and sometimes beautiful – honest, angry and vulnerable, mercifully free of commercial restraints.

If The Smiths' album sleeves had invariably depicted images and idols from Morrissey's past, in this respect he would henceforth only look towards the future by utilizing photographs of himself, each seemingly more attractive than the last – on *Viva Hate* there are two studio shots by Anton Corbin, who several years later would produce videos for Depeche Mode.

The album opens with 'Alsatian Cousin', a roisterous affair thought to have been inspired by Alan Bennett's play, *Forty Years On*, which contains the line 'I was distantly related to the Woolf family through some Alsatian cousins.' 'Little Man, What Now?', a slight slant on Judy Garland's 'I'm Just An In-Between', with its 'too old to be a child star/ too young to take leads' theme, was also the title of a German post-war novel by Hans Fallada, subsequently filmed, though much of the song's content comes from one of Denis Norden's *Looks Familiar* television programmes – the 'nervous juvenile' is said to have been Jack Wilde, who played the Artful Dodger in the film version of *Oliver!*

Critics were unanimous in their opinion that, both lyrically and musically, 'Everyday is Like Sunday' is the most classic, accomplished song on the album, taking full advantage of the lush, six-piece string section headed by Fenella Baton on violin. Years before, the poet laureate, Sir John Betjeman had recorded his impressions of a provincial town in 'Slough', a poem containing the then potentially danger-ous line 'Come, friendly bombs, and fall on Slough'; Morrissey's own gaze fell on 'a seaside town they forgot to close down' – and who has not experienced the misery of such a place during an out-of-season sojourn, searching for something to do, or merely for sustenance and 'greased tea'?

The song was released as a single in June 1988, and reached number 9 in the hit-parade. Chrissie Hynde, the singer with The Pretenders (soon to be joined by Johnny Marr) liked it so much that she decided at once to record a cover-version. Even so, Morrissey's overwhelming gratitude towards those fans whose loyalty had pushed his first two singles into the Top 10 did not prevent him from voicing his opinions during an interview at the Cadogan Hotel in Chelsea – in the actual room which had witnessed the arrest of Oscar Wilde in April 1895 – about the sheer mediocrity of the hit-parade. Suggesting that the charts could only have been rigged, he added, 'I don't believe that certain people are going out and buying certain records in the Top 10.' His response, when asked what he thought of rap, was, 'I really do think it's a great musical stench. I find it very offensive, artless and styleless. To me it's very reminiscent of . . . pop thuggery.'

Two of the songs from *Viva Hate* caused tremendous controversy – one immediately, another four years later – and no small amount of ill-feeling amongst anti-Morrissey cliques. 'Margaret on the Guillotine', it was revealed, had been one of the original working titles for The Smiths' 'The Queen is Dead' album. And if Morrissey's earlier call for another Sirhan Sirhan had failed to attract a suitable 'mar-tyr' to his cause, records, he defended, were there for ever. Thus the much-repeated line 'When will you die?' followed by the polite request '*Please* die . . . make the dream real', stirred up considerable passion particularly amongst the gay community who were virulently opposed to the infamous Clause 28. 'I find the Thatcher syndrome very stressful and evil,' Morrissey told Shaun Philips of *Sounds*. 'The most perfect example is Clause 28. I think that embodies Thatcher's very nature and her quite natural hatred ... I think that's been the story throughout her reign, so I don't see the point of wandering around Marble Arch in a pink T-shirt, carrying books by Andrea Dworkin.' Across the Channel, the French star Renaud had been inspired to write 'Miss Maggie', a Morrisseyian pamphlet which he had set to music and performed with a variety of *trucs* or devices – weaving numerous filthy epithets into his propagandist tapestry, and ending his song with scenes of mock-urination, enabling it to top the French hit-parade for several months. Only Morrissey, however, could make a potentially nasty topic sound incurably romantic – even the swish of the guillotine at the very end did nothing to detract from this. The French journalist who compared 'Miss Maggie' with 'Margaret on the Guillotine' said of the latter, 'It has probably the most definitive ending to a dramatic song since the shattered glass in Piaf's "Amants d'un Jour".'

In the same interview, Morrissey was called to defend his decision to record 'Bengali in Platforms', previously taped as a demo with a different melody at the time of The Smiths' split, with the guitarist Ivor Perry, who was being considered as a replacement for Johnny Marr. The song presented Morrissey with a classic 'shoot the messenger' dilemma, and brought renewed 'racist' tags from the tabloids though in fact, setting aside those misconceptions arising from a lack of comprehension and intelligence when analysing any piece of dramatic verse, Morrissey's lyrics may be deemed decidedly *anti*-racist, for it is the narrator who has been given the task of advising the immigrant to shelve his western plans because 'life is hard enough when you belong here' – which he does with great compassion as the descendant of immigrants himself. Morrissey explained, 'There are many people who are so obsessed with racism that one can't mention the word Bengali . . . even if you're saying "Bengali, marry me",' he protested – and, unwittingly foreseeing another grave human rights issue, added, 'If you went to Yugoslavia tomorrow, you'd probably feel that you didn't belong *there.*' Some months later, a journalist – no doubt wishing to avoid being tarred with the same brush – ventured the criticism that others before him had so obviously failed to delve behind the feelings of Morrissey's songs, only to bring the acerbic comment, 'I think we have to assume that journalists do actually try. I mean, a lot of them aren't massively equipped upstairs . . . they get the spade out and try to dig, but can't quite manage it.'

The compulsion to shed the skin of one's unhappy youth and genuinely look towards the future was the topic of perhaps the only truly optimistic song on the album. Masterfully slotted between 'Suedehead' and 'The Ordinary Boys', whose subjects are content with their unambitious backstreet lives, was the startlingly melodic 'Break Up the Family', in which love is able to conquer hopelessness once one leaves the parental nest.

Self-deprecation is the subject of several songs. 'I Don't Mind if You Forget Me' contains the familiar put-down 'never left an impression on anyone' and concludes that if rejection is one thing, then 'rejection from a fool is cruel'. 'Dial-a-Cliché' is reminiscent of the frequently bullying 'do-as-I-do' tactics of Northern parenthood, and 'Angel, Angel, Down We Go Together' reverses the roles by displaying the singer's support and inner strength as he dissuades a friend from committing suicide. Equally disturbing, and lyrically more complex, is 'Late Night, Maudlin Street', a long song which one reviewer described as nakedly autobiographical. *Late Night on Watling Street* was the title of a collection of short stories by Bill Naughton, while Maudlin Street was the name of the problem school in *Carry On Teacher*. Although there are a few postcard quips – notably 'Me – without clothes? Well, a nation turns its back and gags!' – the general tone is devastatingly morose, almost as if the narrator is attempting to erase once and for all not just his unhappy past, but the projected misery of a lifetime by leaving the house he loathes.

In the wake of this portentous song Morrissey admitted, perhaps ruefully, 'Youth for me was revolting – feeling young, I always hated that. I feel a *bit* better as I stumble towards middle age.' At around this time, too, he condescended to do an interview with Paul Morley, one-time manager of Frankie Goes to Hollywood, which was published in the March edition of *Blitz* under the heading; 'Wilde Child'. The lengthy piece, still regarded by many Morrissey fans as the interviewer's finest, bearing in mind the interviewee's fondness for prevarication and surprise, began with Morley stating:

> Morrissey is as I've always wanted to imagine him – a silly blend of the ordinary and the delightfully ostentatious. His talent is sufficiently exquisite and perverse for me to consider him a truly great writer. I am not put off even when he is at his most contrived. Morrissey also makes me laugh, as if his life has been him acting out his own violent comedy . . . I am very moved by his transformation from utter loser to shy playboy of frustration.

Morley's questions bordered somewhere betwixt the sublime and the downright audacious, hardly surprising, perhaps, when Morrissey greeted him with a coy 'The last time we met, we romped naked together at playschool' – after which the journalist took the bull by the horns and posed the question, 'How did you move from being the village idiot to being the gangleader?' –all in all, almost a Hedda Hopper versus Louella Parsons debate which worked remarkably well. Comments like 'Being selfish is the first step towards maturity', 'If I hadn't found my social position when I was a teenager so amusing, I would have strangled myself', and 'I'm not very good at being dull' slipped off Morrissey's tongue so glibly that he could have been accused of reading them from cue-cards, which of course he was not. Apprehensions and fears, too, were discussed openly and honestly.

> I'm still in the position that when the window cleaner calls, I have to go into another room than the one he is cleaning . . . I feel like a bespectacled six-year-old. When the doorbell rings, my automatic response is to hide or run away . . . they might want you to do something you don't want to do. It's one of those trivial obsessive fears, like being on an airplane, I always feel that I have to be racked by physical fear, and if I am I'll arrive safe. I feel if I relax, drink a whisky, converse, the plane will crash. I have to be in total turmoil, or the plane won't make it. The terrifying thing is, as you get older it doesn't get any easier. Fears just seem to cement into place.

The now essential 'tabloid ingredients' of sex and sexuality also formed part of Morley's agenda, giving way to a number of vulgar questions which the singer handled remarkably well. When asked if there was any sex in Morrissey, he replied, 'None whatsoever, which in itself is quite sexy. In a particular sense, I'm a virgin . . . I've always felt above sex and love because all the emotions I need to express come from within myself.'

Morrissey's obvious charm and appealing way of discussing even the most personal topic was, in the world of popular music, refreshing when compared to some of the views being expressed in contemporaneous interviews by former friends and colleagues. Pete Burns of Dead Or Alive, never one to mince words, readily pointed out to his journalist pal Kris Kirk that he had taken to sharing hotel bedrooms with his wife *and* one of the musicians from his band, explaining, 'That way I can give it or take it, depending on the mood I'm in. It was always my ambition to form a homo band.' In another interview with the same journalist, The Smiths' former go-go dancer James Maker, whose own rococo band Raymonde had recently folded, went one step further by admitting that he had slept with both his managers because he had adopted the maxim 'Begin with your managers and screw your way up the hierarchy'. Maker also confessed that he had starred in two Swedish gay-porn movies – one, *Bike Boys Go Ape*, had subsequently become an under-the-counter 'classic'. Such outbursts, however, left Kris Kirk unmoved and his response was, 'In a world where stars are too often pigeon-holed, my candidate for sainthood is Morrissey, who artistically and morally is streets ahead of these people. He sets out to be a decent man, and he succeeds because this is exactly what he is.'

In September 1988, whilst Morrissey was riding high on the crest of his very individual post-Smiths wave, Geoff Travis of Rough Trade released *Rank*, the company's final contractual obligation to The Smiths – a 'live' recording of their concert at the Kilburn National Ballroom on 23 October 1986, when the group had been augmented on second guitar by Craig Gannon. The fact that Morrissey – who whittled the 21-song set down to just fourteen, and co-designed the Alexandra Bastedo sleeve with Jo Slee and Caryn Gough – included Johnny Marr's instrumental 'The Draize Train' was doubtless his way of saying 'no hard feelings' to his still errant former partner, who because of the decision was ensured the lion's share of the songwriting royalties – no small amount, for *Rank* reached number 2 in the album charts.

In October 1988, The Smiths' legendary *Peel Session* was released on the Strange Fruit label, though the proposed solo session, though recorded, was dismissed by Morrissey as 'horrible', and never saw the light of day. Morrissey blamed

insensitive technicians at the Maida Vale studios for failing
to treat him with the respect he deserved, adding bitterly,
'They were quite accustomed to treat everyone like an
insignificant, unsigned group from Poole.' He also readily
pointed out that his first two singles had reached the Top 10
without the aid of concerts, television appearances, and the
now obligatory promotional video. On the eve of the release
of *Viva Hate* he had said, in contempt of so-called pop senil-
ity, 'I don't want to walk on stage with a hair transplant,
with shoes on the wrong feet. I don't want to haul the car-
cass across the studio floor and reach for the bath-chair as I
put down the vocal' – a strange statement from a young man
of 27, with many years of his career still ahead of him. Now,
however, when asked if he had made any plans for the
future, his response – 'None whatsoever!' – sent shock waves
of grave despondency amongst his legion of disciples.

6

Not a Thin, Swirling Creature Any More

On 22 December 1988, the Civic Hall in Wolverhampton – in the world of British showbusiness just an ordinary, run-of-the-mill venue with no particular claim to fame – was witness to some of the most emotional scenes ever viewed on a provincial stage. The occasion was Morrissey's first concert appearance in two years, announced by the star himself as 'Me saying goodbye'.

For thousands of fans who, having seen nothing of their idol since six months before the break-up of The Smiths, had truly believed *Viva Hate* to be a one-off before Morrissey committed himself prematurely to history but not to oblivion, there were many thousands more who predicted that Wolverhampton would prove the beginning of a new Smiths era. Johnny Marr had been swallowed up by a new, lucrative but not unexpectedly less famous career – having just played on The Pretenders' *Windows of the World*, The The's *The Beat(en) Generation*, as well as their about-to-be released *Mind Bomb* album – and even a congratulatory postcard from Marr to his former partner failed to heal the hurts of the past. Importantly, however, the re-emergence of Andy Rourke, Craig Gannon and Mike Joyce rekindled a spark of hope – fanned into a massively optimistic flame by the eve of the actual performance – that The Smiths were about to re-form. This rumour was the main topic of conversation among the long line of fans who had made the pilgrimage from all over the country – some of whom had camped out or slept in the backs of trucks and vans for three days, mindless of the cold and no small amount of unwarranted police harassment – to pay homage to the man they loved. James Brown of the *New Musical Express* compared the alternating outbreaks of hysteria and despondency with the picket-lines of 'battered British mineworkers' during the 1984 strike, and chronicled the event as having 'already gone down in rock and roll history alongside Bowie at his most androgynous, The Beatles and Stones at their most popular, The Pistols at their most threatening' – and he was not wrong.

There was also another reason for the Wolverhampton concert. Some of the crowd scenes outside and inside the theatre were filmed to highlight a forthcoming showcase video, and the venue itself was to promote Morrissey's new single – 'The Last of the Famous International Playboys' was scheduled to be released in February 1989. Because the performance was to be filmed, the usual audience conditions – complimentary tickets, supplied to local advertisers and dignitaries, and a generally indifferent public who by and large would not have been interested in what was happening on stage – were dispensed with. Morrissey announced that though there would be no cover charge, tickets would only be supplied to those fans who turned up wearing Smiths/Morrissey T-shirts. Needless to say, pandemonium erupted when more than 5,000 admirers besieged the box-office for the 1,700 tickets on offer. Windows were smashed as the disappointed element tried to gatecrash side entrances, barriers were crushed, the police brought in dogs, and the town centre was eventually closed to traffic. Adjacent to the theatre was parked a Blood Transfusion van, and a compound housing several retired pit donkeys. The spirit of Christmas was further evoked by the blaring speakers of ghetto-blasters playing seasonable songs by Bing Crosby and Ruby Murray. Other scenes were reminiscent of a medieval sideshow – jugglers, Morrissey soundalikes, and one young man who displayed a talent for eating daffodils!

The hero's arrival was suitably humble, in a 1950s green and cream Vista schoolbus, almost a replica of the one used in the film *The Belles of St Trinian's*. Later he confessed that the vehicle had broken down twice en route to the theatre, adding sardonically, 'I had a driver, he also broke down. It was typical of Old England to let me down!'

On stage, Morrissey revealed a hunkier than usual physique through a diaphanous black shirt, traditionally the emblem of the realist entertainers, and the deafening applause greeting his appearance on stage lasted almost as long as his first song, The Smiths' 'Stop Me if You've Heard This One Before'. His set was relatively short, just seven songs, but each effortlessly transformed into a histrionic event. He exposed his breast (or maybe more likely offered his heart) during 'Sister, I'm a Poet' and 'Sweet and Tender Hooligan', invited stage invasions hardly ever enjoyed by rock predecessors for the new single/theme song and 'Interesting Drug', wallowed in *Strangeways* nostalgia with 'Death at One's Elbow', and, with the title of one song, mirrored the feelings of those many hundreds of fans left stamping their feet in the cold streets of the town – though 'Disappointed' does contain several chilling lines that they might not have cherished on so auspicious an occasion, particularly when he pronounced, 'This is the last song I will ever sing!'

Morrissey said afterwards, extolling the talents of 'torch' singers of the Garland-Bassey mould whose souls were invariably laid bare before the footlights, 'I like to think a singer is singing with a sense of immediate death. The Gallows Humour, lah-de-dah. I like a singer to sing with desperation ... I find people who are steeped in plunging depression rapturously interesting and if I saw an individual smothered in flowers, I'd have to run up to him. Happiness is still something to be attained. I don't think I know anyone who is truly happy. I suppose it's worth waiting for.'

As might be expected, there was hardly a dry eye in the

house. At times Morrissey himself seemed on the verge of tears, and the overwhelming waves of sentiment must have been felt by Stephen Street, watching his songs being performed in public for the very first time, savouring every response. Vocally, Morrissey was not at his best because of the repeated stage invasions by fans who wanted to congratulate, embrace, or merely touch – as one observer told me, 'It can't be easy, trying to sing in tune which you've got five hundred pounds of writhing flesh weighing down on you!' Simon Reynolds of the *Observer* described him not less perfectly, but more prosaically as 'a paradigm of a certain ethereal, inhibited masculinity which would rather live in dreams than risk being disappointed by reality', though in effect this occasion was a dream come true. Morrissey later admitted, 'It wasn't an attention-seeking device. I just needed to see some particular faces. It was immensely uplifting, practically medical . . . it would have been nice to complete a song without interruption, but for some reason it just didn't matter. The night went for me beyond performing. It was something else.'

'The Last of the Famous International Playboys' was released in February 1989, entering the hit-parade with such gusto that even the *New Musical Express* proclaimed it would give Morrissey his first number 1. It was coupled with 'Lucky Lisp', the title an alleged pun on that of 'Lucky Lips', originally recorded in May 1959 (the month and year of Morrissey's birth) by the American star Gale Storm, and revived some years later by Cliff Richard. It is hard to tell from Morrissey's ambiguous lines 'When your talent becomes apparent/I will roar from the stalls/ . . . The Saints smile shyly down on you' whether he is praising Cliff Richard or scoffing. 'Michael's Bones', which appeared on the 12-inch, is another song about the Moors Murders which thankfully did not attract the same attention as the last one.

The fact that 'The Last of the Famous International

Playboys' stalled at number 6 in the charts did not stop it
from becoming an instant standard, a firm favourite with
fans and henceforth an essential ingredient of his stage-
shows, yet, in effect, like its chart predecessor, a song which
only Morrissey may rightfully perform without attracting
criticism of the severest kind. Although the title is probably
not seriously intended to be Morrissey's image of himself
after years of self-disapproval, many thousands of wishful-
thinking fans refused to believe that such a description could
apply to anyone *but* him, particularly when he announced
with unabashed flair, 'The Last of the Famous International
Playboys are Bowie, Bolan, Devoto and me. I think I must
be, absolutely, a total sex object in every sense of the word.
A lot of men and a lot of women find me unmistakably
attractive . . . it amuses me, and a lot of the male followers
who are, as far as the eye can see, natural specimens, have
very very anguished and devilishly rabid desires in my direc-
tion. I find that quite historic.'

In fact, the theme of the song – one of criminal idolatry, in
this instance the effect of the Kray Twins' dark deeds on an
impressionable society and the way in which that society had
virtually turned them into celebrities – had been used before.
Morrissey drew comparisons between it and The Smiths'
'Shoplifters of the World Unite'.

Tim Broad's promotional film for the song features
Morrissey and his ex-Smiths musicians performing against a
green backdrop, which most realists would have shunned
like the plague, alternating with footage of the 'hero in
prison' – not Reggie Kray, but the archetypal bedsit adolescent who, when not studying the Elvis Presley/Jack
Nicholson memorabilia on his wall, catches up on his box-
ing lessons so necessary for his precarious outings into the
streets of Bermondsey. The young actor was Jason Rush,
who appeared in *The Two of Us*, Roger Tonge's controversial film about teenage gay acceptance – later he played an
extension of the character in BBC1's *EastEnders*. Though he

was becoming used to appearing on celluloid, Morrissey was still not enthusiastic, saying, 'If I didn't, I would disappear off the face of the earth. If I didn't work with Tim I'd be in turmoil. I could not make what the dilly-dally world calls a video.'

By March 1989, when Morrissey's career was reaching almost unprecedented heights, the music press reported rumours of a serious rift between himself and Stephen Street, exacerbated by the producer's sudden decision to have an injunction put on 'Interesting Drug', which EMI had announced would be Morrissey's next single. Though it was difficult to separate truth from hearsay, the main source of the problem appears to have been financial, and it did place a strain on the partnership. Added to this was the polite but nevertheless ongoing wrangle with Craig Gannon, and renewed efforts by Andy Rourke and Mike Joyce – in spite of the amiable ambiance of Wolverhampton – demanding a slice of Smithdom which proved something of a non-starter because The Smiths, contractually at least, did not extend beyond Morrissey and Johnny Marr who had rightfully and legally shared songwriting royalties, and taken 40 per cent of the mechanical royalties (revenues largely accrued from record sales) leaving the other 20 per cent to be shared by the rhythm section. Morrissey and Marr came up with what they hoped might have proved the ideal solution, ten per cent of the group's basic royalties, but this was rejected. Gannon consulted a lawyer, took the pair to the High Court, and several months later was awarded substantial damages. An irate Morrissey condemned this as 'an outrage of public justice', adding, 'Everybody involved knew he didn't have a leg to stand on, yet, through some perversion of justice, he walked away with £42,000. But my opinion is that Craig Gannon didn't really win because he's *still* Craig Gannon. Ha!' Some two years later, Andy Rourke changed his mind and settled out of court, but Mike Joyce pressed on with his claim, instigating legal proceedings and declaring, 'There was no deal finalized as far as I as concerned. I was just swept along by the excitement of it all. I was happy to be in the band, that was enough.' What is remarkable is that all three musicians appear to have been on friendly terms with Morrissey and Marr, who still had neither spoken nor met since The Smiths' split.

Stephen Street lifted his injunction, and 'Interesting Drug' was released in April 1989, reaching number 9 in the charts. It is a bright, bouncy piece, augmented by Kirsty MacColl on backing vocals. On the B-side is 'Such a Little Thing Makes Such a Big Difference' which contains the now classic observation, 'Most people keep their brains between their legs'. The 12-inch includes 'Sweet and Tender Hooligan', taken from the concert at Wolverhampton, and there is also a rare one-track 12-inch version laser-etched with the words 'MOTOR CYCLE AU PAIR BOY' and featuring a picture of Oscar Wilde clutching a sunflower. Even rarer is the promotional disc, labelled 'SPM 29' – the initials and age of the artiste. Though Morrissey is thought to have actually considered becoming an au pair during his teens, the inspiration for the title came from Motorcycle Boy, one of the characters in the cult American film *Rumblefish*.

Tim Broad's spellbinding film-vignette for 'Interesting Drug' caused quite a stir, cleverly combining *Carry On* humour with anti-government propaganda. Even the setting evokes a return to the Maudlin Street of *Carry On Teacher*, flavoured with the rooftops of *Coronation Street*. The fictitious Hawtrey High School for Boys becomes a base for attacking not just animal cruelty, but the unemployment crisis and Norman Tebbit's much-criticized statement to England's state dependants, 'Get on your bike and find yourself a job!' The busty actress Diane Alton is seen chaining herself and her bicycle to the school railings as the camera zooms in to pick up the manufacturer's logo, CHOPPER. Inside the school, the hunkier than usual sixth-formers lounge around reading the *New Musical Express*, complete with

Diana Dors cover, scrawl slogans on lavatory walls, and strut around wearing women's high-heeled shoes. The graffiti, 'THERE ARE SOME BAD PEOPLE ON THE RIGHT, *almost* the opening line of the song, is seen before the pupils go off to the playground, where Morrissey is handing out animal-liberation leaflets. Henceforth, led by a Bunny Girl, a raid is conducted on the school laboratory from which the animals are set free. Morrissey's point is hammered home by scenes of seal-clubbing and anti-fur posters. The former, and the wording of the graffiti, caused a national outcry and the BBC announced that they would not be showing the film. For once the *New Musical Express* actually supported Morrissey: Danny Kelly urged fans, 'Whip out your "Street is Murder" promotional quill *now*, dash off a series of letters to EMI and all the TV companies and demand to see it *today*!' The film was eventually broadcast on *Top of the Pops*, and when the song appeared on Morrissey's next album the word 'right' had been changed to 'rise' – not that this prevented him from proclaiming, 'The bad people on the *rise* are the willing students of Tebbit.'

Morrissey's immense success in Britain did not go unnoticed overseas, but, as usual, Morrissey's patriotism was infinitely more powerful than the lure of the almighty dollar. In a series of revealing, candid interviews with James Brown of the *New Musical Express*, Morrissey was perfectly willing to risk casting caution to the wind by hitting out at the de-Anglification of his country and its 'decreasing contemporary reference points'.

The generations of people who made England such a fascinating, interesting and artistically gentle place are slipping away. We're almost at a stage when there won't be anyone living who can remember the Second World War. Even the English language, I find, has been hopelessly mucked about with and everything is American or Australian. It's not that I dislike America – America is fine on the other side of the Atlantic. It works quite well and it's interesting. If Margaret Thatcher was a strong person – which she isn't – she would not allow this Americanization to happen.

Neither was Morrissey particularly anxious to rush off to Europe. In the same interview he suggested that his extraordinarily loving relationship with his admirers owed much to his reluctance to tour abroad. 'I despise travelling by air, surface and sea, so I'm stranded. I'm not going to pop up in some greasy Greek festival, or at some waterlogged field in Belgium. I'm not going to be photographed backstage in the Greek Ampitheatre with Yoko Ono and Art Garfunkel,' he said.

Although Greece had yet to fall under Morrissey's spell, there were a number of complaints from aggrieved Belgian fans. One, from a young man named Christophe Devos, received a personal, very pleasant reply from Morrissey himself. Written on the back of a postcard, and thanking the fan for 'kind words' which had been anything but, it concluded with 'Belgium is *so far away*!' 'It did not make my day, but it made my whole *life*!' Christophe later told me.

Equally strange, for a time at least, was Morrissey's reluctance to perform in his homeland. Much of the summer of 1989 was spent writing songs and listening to music sent to him by fans, though even this was not always readily appreciated by one whose tastes were so particular. As he said, 'I get sent a lot of records and tapes which I spin aimlessly, then into the bin they go.'

Following his disagreement with Stephen Street, Morrissey put himself in the capable hands of a new production team. Clive Langer and Alan Winstanley had achieved recognition in their work with Madness and Elvis Costello, and before them Blue Rondo A La Turk in the early eighties. The pair part-owned Hook End Manor Studios, near Reading, a former Tudor monastery not too far from the infamous jail which had for a while housed Oscar Wilde, and it was from this base towards the end of 1989 that Morrissey began developing his new album. In the November, EMI released a single, 'Ouija Board, Ouija Board', coupled with 'Yes, I am Blind', a Morrissey poem set to Andy Rourke's music, and on the 12-inch a cover-version of Herman's Hermits' old hit, 'East West'.

The new song peaked at number 18 in the charts, and though its death-orientated cynicism sailed above the heads of staid British critics who, in spite of a near-decade of Morrisseyisms still had not caught up with their European counterparts when it came to analysing lyrics, it did not deserve to be hammered by the music press. Nick Kent, in an interview which Morrissey later attacked for the way it had been transcribed for readers of *The Face*, called it 'numbingly bad'. A better description of the work comes from Siobhan Fahey, one half of the defunct Shakespear's Sister who had taken their name (misspelt) from The Smiths' song, who said, 'Like so many Morrissey songs it evokes two reactions – the melody is gut-wrenchingly sad, but the words hysterically funny.'

The narrator is lamenting the death of a friend who has left 'the Unhappy Planet with all the carnivores and destructors on it', and attempts to reach her in the next world with the help of a medium and board – with disappointing results, after spelling out S-T-E-V-E-N, it tells him to P-U-S-H O double F!

Tim Broad's promotional film for 'Ouija Board, Ouija Board' features Kathy Burke, and the comedy actress Joan Sims as the deranged medium. It was shot in the garden of Morrissey's home in the opulent suburb of Bowden. Joan Sims was madly enthusiastic about her work with the singer, and praised his ripe sense of humour, adding, 'I was totally unprepared for what I was letting myself in for. I was treated like a princess all day. If ever you want a CV on my *Carry Ons*, he knows them better than I do. He's a very brainy

chap. I hate to call him a pop star because it's such a horrible word. He's a very nice gentleman.' For a number of
years, Morrissey had been attempting to lure another
famous *Carry On* star, the bespectacled Charles Hawtrey,
out of retirement to appear in one of Broad's films, without
success, but Joan Sims had not even hesitated. Standing next
to her, he said, was for him the greatest moment of the year.
'She was so enormously gifted,' he went on. 'And here was
I, a silly sausage from somewhere near Manchester.'
Morrissey himself could become quite savage towards anyone who had the audacity to call him a pop star, and said to
James Brown of the *New Musical Express*, 'I am as a figure
more popular than ever, but I'd gag before I'd use the word
"pop star".'

'Ouija Board, Ouija Board', ludicrously perhaps when one
considers the comedy element of the accompanying film,
received ferocious criticism not just from the media, but
from the Church, who accused Morrissey of inciting impressionable fans towards involvement with the occult. His
response, in which he vented his spleen on the newspaper
which had branded him 'Devil Worshipper' was: 'The only
contact I ever made with the dead was when I spoke to a
journalist from the *Sun*.' Some time later, when discussing
the song on a New York radio show, he spoke of the British
'do-or-dare' practice known as 'Twelve O'Clock Handle',
explaining, 'If you stare into a mirror at midnight in a completely darkened room with a candle below your face, your
face supposedly changes into the face of somebody who has
died and who wants to reach you.' He then expressed his
contempt for cynics and 'non-believers' adding, 'It's a very,
very private thing, and I think it depends on how open or
sensitive you are. If you're closed, nothing comes to you.'

On 9 February 1990 – the day after what would have been
James Dean's 59th birthday, as one fan observed – Morrissey
arrived in Los Angeles for a brief visit. He was invited to
appear on KROQ radio, arguably the city's most prestigious

'alternative' station. Depeche Mode had similarly been launched in the United States at a radio-party in San Francisco, following which they never looked back. Outside the KROQ building, a thousand fans rushed Morrissey's car, and security officials – always a bigger problem on both sides of the Atlantic than over-enthusiastic admirers – became concerned. In fact, these fans could not have been kinder or more affectionate, and some photographs of the event reveal Morrissey close to tears.

Most of the questions had been asked before – Band Aid, vegetarianism, the fur-trade, and witchcraft. When asked if he would welcome the opportunity to work once more with Johnny Marr he replied, 'I would, instantly. But I don't think he wants to. So life goes on.' One problem which was no different on this side of the Atlantic than it was back home was the acute lack of airplay given to Morrissey's records – as one disc jockey put it, 'It's not easy, fitting "Late Night, Maudlin Street" between Madonna and Janet Jackson.' Morrissey was asked on air, 'Is there a place in Morrissey's world of pop music for people such as Madonna and Janet Jackson?' In the past, the Material Girl had been labelled 'the nearest one can get towards organized prostitution'. Now, he levelled, 'Madonna I think is slightly different because I think she's proven herself to be quite an independent, individual person. Janet Jackson, as far as I am concerned, has no talent at all.'

The officials at KROQ immediately adopted Morrissey as a 'foundation artiste' – an honour approaching beatitude in the American radio world – promoting each of his records with bumper extravaganzas, car-stickers, posters, calendars and all manner of memorabilia. There was also an admirable boom on Smithdom – within months, most of their albums would go gold, selling in excess of 500,000 copies each. The ultimate accolade however, in direct contrast to some of the gratuitous insults being delivered only too readily by the British music press, came from an anonymous journalist who wrote, 'When words aren't enough to describe the way someone else's words set to music make you feel, you know you're dealing with a genius.'

In England, however, one type of fan was causing his idol no small amount of discomfort and, according to Morrissey, setting a very bad example. In March 1990 Jim White of the *Independent*, aided by a fan named Robert Graham whose play about The Smiths had recently been performed at Manchester's Contact Theatre, and a young man named Eliot Marks who in August 1988 had begun organizing annual Smiths conventions – the first of which had attracted 1200 visitors from all corners of the globe – conducted a journalistic tour of Morrissey's Manchester. White's lengthy, enthralling feature included a map, and photographs of the Southern Cemetery, the Salford Lads Club complete with portal graffiti, and the tour took in Strangeways Prison, Boddington's Brewery, the Factory Club and the Hacienda, Whalley Range, and some of the seedier aspects of Hulme which may not have pleased or impressed Morrissey, whose first compilation video, punned *Hulmerist*, was about to be released.

Neither did the singer approve of Eliot Marks's unconventional method of recruiting adherents to the Morrissey banner. Subsequent conventions were held in Tokyo, Los Angeles, and Paris – at Le Locomotif, a gay club in the red-light district, at which the organizer issued a proclamation that 'all moneys raised by conventions past and present will go to a charity of Morrissey's choice'. Morrissey hotly denied giving it his blessing and took the not unusual step of issuing a threat of legal action. The fans at the Parisian venue retaliated by allowing themselves to be browbeaten into signing a petition, part of which read: 'Discos around this country laugh when we request your music, so we need somewhere where we can all come together away from all this music that's destroying our country. Please give us your blessing to hold further events, share it with others . . . life is

not worth living without the music to cling to.'
Notwithstanding, Morrissey refused to capitulate, and a
statement was issued by his press-office reading: 'Morrissey
objects to this type of profiteering because he doesn't want
his fans to be exploited.'

Morrissey was still working at Hook End Studios on his
new album, which had been given the title *Bona Drag*, and
he was very enthusiastic about it during the first few months
of the year. One of the scheduled songs, 'Get off the Stage',
recounts a pet horror, that of rock-senility. During his trip to
America he had been appalled by the 'geriatric content' of
the Billboard charts, graced by such stalwarts as The
Grateful Dead, Eric Clapton, Bob Dylan and The Rolling
Stones. He commented on the latter, 'I've been so disgusted
by their most recent comeback that I no longer find it sad or
pitiful . . . just immense anger that they don't just *get out of
the way*!' Another song, 'Striptease with a Difference', tells
of the manipulation required in a game of strip poker so as
to lose, and remove one's clothes. The former song was subsequently released. The latter, along with several others, was
taped, but the album in its anticipated form never saw the
light of day, for whatever reason. Len Brown, who interviewed Morrissey for *Vox*, may have been justified in pointing out that 'Things seemed to reach a post-Smiths low
when, following what he describes as a "condemning, disgraceful interview" in *The Face* – "*I could tell you things
about Nick Kent that would take the frizz out of your Afro!*"
– he seemed to scrap his *Bona Drag* studio album overnight.'

One song which did emerge from the Hook End Manor
sessions was the Morrissey/Armstrong collaboration, 'He
Knows I'd Love to See Him', which, once he has dismissed
his childhood abode as 'the arse of the world', deals with the
aftermath of his verbal attacks on Margaret Thatcher, when
he had actually been questioned by the police and accused of
being 'Just another fool with radical views'.

This song was one of the six salvaged from Morrissey's

cancelled album which EMI had designated for release as his next two singles. Then backing vocals were provided by the Canadian chanteuse Mary Margaret O'Hara, who had recently completed her first British tour. Morrissey had just listened to her latest album, *Miss America*, and one track in particular, 'Year in Song', had made a deep impression on him: 'I hadn't in a decade heard someone singing because of a deep-set personal neurosis, absolute need and desperation. You'd think she might fall apart at any second and become a pile of rags and bones on stage.'

O'Hara also backed Morrissey on 'November Spawned a Monster', an immensely bold, moving pastiche which wrenches every emotion contained within the Morrissey frame. The recording, coupled with 'He Knows I'd Love to See Him' and 'The Girl Least Likely To', was released in April 1990 and peaked at number 12 in the charts. Morrissey's instructions to O'Hara had been explicit: 'I went into the vocal booth and said, "Just simply give birth", which she most expertly did, whilst I stood behind with a mop and bucket.' In his own words, the song told of those limitations imposed on a wheelchair-bound young woman whose ambition is to walk down the street wearing clothes she has gone out to buy for herself. Morrissey has the quality of being able to understand the feelings of one less fortunate than himself by climbing inside that person's skin. The song drew comparisons with the earlier 'Girlfriend in a Coma' in that the narrator alternates devotion ('Oh, hug me! Oh, hug me!') with anger and contempt ('Dream of love/ Because it's the closest you will ever get to love') in his attempts to come to terms with his subject's plight. This is exactly what happens, of course, in many such real-life situations, though many of Morrissey's critics were not slow in claiming that lines such as 'If the lights were out/ Could you even bear to kiss her on the mouth?' were a direct and deliberate mockery of the afflicted, delivered only in the poorest taste. Nothing could have been further from the truth.

Though Morrissey did confess that 'November Spawned a Monster' was his version of The New York Dolls' 'Frankenstein', he did add the important point – and was acknowledged for doing so by a large number of disabled fans – that 'If you're perceptive and sensitive you can fully imagine the lifelong frustrations of constantly being discussed, constantly having people being irritatingly kind to you.'

Tim Broad's promotional film for 'November Spawned a Monster' is generally regarded as the finest piece of Morrissey's art ever captured on celluloid. Filmed in all his vibrant glory at Mushroom Rock, in the desolate sun-scorched Death Valley, and clad in a black diaphanous creation which is neither shirt nor blouse, he preens, struts, prostrates himself, writhes, thrusts, agonizes, explores his body, and almost seems to give birth. After years of self-deprecation and self-mockery, this stunning display of muscular anguish becomes a definitive study of narcissism which only Morrissey could have been capable of getting away with without overplaying the theme. On the Continent, critics made favourable comparisons with the death throes of the Resistance fighter in the famous Wajda film, *Ashes and Diamonds*, and with reason – Zbigniew Cybulsky, the star of the film, has always been regarded as the 'Polish James Dean', and when the Morrissey film was first broadcast on Polish television, the singer was hailed as the 'British Cybulsky'.

Morrissey's next enterprise, and one in which he used all his vernacular skills, involved the transfer of his persona from the wheelchair to the proclivities of the London rent-boy, as depicted in documentaries such as *Johnny, Go Home*. *Polari*, a Romany word which roughly translates as 'the joy of being incomprehensible', was a form of communication popular amongst the London gay fraternity of the early sixties, particularly in the Earls Court and Piccadilly areas where it is thought to have been developed at the turn of the century by contemporaries of Oscar Wilde. It was then effectively the only way of sizing up a client without attracting too much attention from bystanders, who might have been shocked by such things, and its subsequent revival owed much to the antics of Julian and Sandy, two gay characters – the very first to feature on British mainstream radio – in the comedy series *Round the Horne*.

The Polari term for homosexual is *omi-polone* (man-woman), a word which often crops up in biographies of Oscar Wilde. Other plum phrases include 'Dolly basket, naff lucoddi!' ('Lovely crotch, shame about the body!') which, thankfully, was not among the phrases Morrissey used in his song 'Piccadilly Palare' (which includes *eek*, 'face'; *riah*, 'hair'; *bona*, 'good'; *varda*, 'looks'). Even so, to the 'uninitiated and ignorant' – in other words, those sections of the public and media who had failed or refused to scratch beneath the surface of his articulate lyricism and realize that he was but interpreting yet another role – the song was regarded with contempt and awarded a definite thumbs-down. The fans, who of course were the only ones who mattered, loved it.

The 'rails' in the song are the iron palings separating the London buildings from the pavements, and the 'rack' is The Meat Rack, one of the amusement arcades used by the Dilly Boys as a base for plying their trade. 'Easy meat', of course, is self-explanatory – these were usually the 'easy pickings' sought out by the married men, or 'belted coats' in the song.

The recording of 'Piccadilly Palare', backed with Stephen Street's 'At Amber' and Andy Rourke's 'Get off the Stage', was released in November 1990, and featured a guest appearance by Suggs, the vocalist from Madness. According to some sources, there was no Tim Broad promotional film for this one because EMI considered it non-commercial, though the record did reach number 18 in the charts and has subsequently taken its rightful place amongst other Morrissey classics. Because of its content, however, it also resurrected the seemingly age-old question of Morrissey's sexuality. Back in 1985 he had told *Smash Hits*, 'I don't recognize such terms as heterosexual, homosexual and bisexual . . . these words do great damage. They confuse people, and make them unhappy. I want to do away with them.' *Square Peg* reported along these lines, but a coda was added to Morrissey's statement which read, 'I don't recognize heterosexuality . . . it doesn't exist, and I'm quite convinced that homosexuality does not exist, either.' He also continued to proclaim his celibacy, saying, 'Celibacy? I can't even recommend it. It's just right for me and wrong for the rest of the population.' What many people fail to realize is that the dictionary definition of the word 'celibacy' is 'bound or resolved not to marry', and does not necessarily have anything to do with abstention from sex.

For some, an 'official' statement seemed to be the order of the day, which of course would have served no purpose whatsoever. An interview with Nick Kent brought him close to losing his temper. Richard Smith, writing an otherwise excellent feature for *Gay Times* under the heading MORRISSEY: SAINT OR SINNER? criticized 'Piccadilly Palare' and ventured, 'If you're not gay, then get your hands off our history. You can't steal the very words from our lips just so you can embellish your songs with (pardon the pun) a bit of rough.' Many people assumed too, and quite erroneously, that 'camp' and 'homosexual' were one and the same thing, one double-standard which Morrissey eradicated in his interview with Lawrence Brown of the *New Musical Express*: 'Some people play rugby, some people listen to *Beyond Our Ken* . . . but if we must use categories, I know heterosexual people who have an enormously camp sense of humour . . . highly intellectual, very witty, totally unattainable by most people.'

A superb example of Morrissey's hetero-camp humour had appeared, etched in his very individual handwriting on the flipside of a 1984 flexi-disc version of 'London', taken from the *Rank* album and given away with Rough Trade's magazine. The poem, 'Poppycocteau' – an amalgamation of 'poppycock' and a reference to the sexual preferences of the French poet-playwright Jean Cocteau, into whose skin he had temporarily climbed – read as follows:

> So then I went to Liverpool,
> and got held up outside a
> night club by two merchant
> seamen who said:
> 'give us your money or give
> us your trousers'
> And as I handed them my
> trousers . . .
> (Well, you've got to make the
> Most of Life, haven't you?)

The music press equally criticized Morrissey's failure to get into the actual Top 10 with his last few singles, attributing this to a decline in popularity, which was of course quite nonsensical. The Smiths had never sold as many singles as he had over the last two years, and no one had ever called them uncommercial. Morrissey was still displeased with the apparent lack of airplay given to his records, and was probably not far wrong when he joked that they would be played more if someone wrote the name 'Tina Turner' on the promo-labels. He added that much of what he was doing was reliant on experiment and an element of surprise, continuing, 'I think there was always the danger of trying to give an audience what it wants. It's more interesting to give an audience what it doesn't want.'

7

'And Another Stage I Burst to Cheer . . .'

Morrissey refused to permit the cancellation of his new album to impede his progress, and the compilation released hot on the heels of 'Piccadilly Palare' – retaining the title *Bona Drag*, in keeping with this – reached number 9 in the album charts, its success a deserved kick in the teeth for those cynics who had sneered that his career was on the skids. *Bona Drag* contains a two-year retrospective of singles and B-sides, though 'East West', 'Michael's Bones' and 'At Amber' were sadly omitted. Speaking to Len Brown of the *New Musical Express*, Morrissey expostulated, 'People will view it suspiciously in England but not in the rest of the world where all these funny little singles were never released. They'll remind people that I'm a fairly living person, although I'm not so sure about that myself!'

In an epoch where the hit-parade was temporarily ripe with Mancunian music – The Happy Mondays, New Order, The Stone Roses, 808 State, James, and The Fall were but a few of the artists who had made the charts over the last year – Morrissey was profoundly unimpressed, refusing to equate record sales with talent. He told Len Brown, this time in an interview for *Vox*, 'If I was herded in with these groups, I'd emigrate to Norway. I still have a boring, old-fashioned notion of talent. I don't want to sound like a member of Fleetwood Mac, however hard that may be, but I don't hear a commendable, impressive voice . . . the level of publicity is outrageous, and there are no real honest faces or even minor celebrities. Taste has completely disappeared.'

The release of *Bona Drag* coincided with another reshuffle of the Morrissey cabinet, one side of him which occasionally frustrated but which invariably reaped a harvest of new songs never less than sparkling in their originality. There had also been 'warnings' from the music press that an album of *brand-new* material was long overdue, though the fans themselves were well aware that quality and not quantity had always been Morrissey's forte. In keeping with the legend, lengthy but not *too* lengthy absences from the concert platform had only helped to perpetuate the singer's mystique and allure.

Thus, assisted by a new but again temporary manager, Morrissey was able to enter Hook End Manor Studios and begin work on a new album, confident that this time there would be no hitches. Fachtna O'Ceallaigh had worked with The Boomtown Rats, dismissed by Morrissey at the time of Band Aid as 'a collection of brontosauri', and the Irish singer Sinead O'Connor, whom he admired for her outspokenness. For a while, Morrissey had been on the lookout for a compatible songwriting partner. A likely candidate had been Tom Verlaine, the legendary American guitarist, who had played with the group Television until their demise in 1979, and it was believed at the time that Verlaine refused to work with Morrissey only because of his unorthodox method of adding lyrics to pre-recorded tapes. The problem was effectively solved when O'Ceallaigh introduced him to a young Bristol-born songwriter-musician named Mark E Nevin.

Like Morrissey, Nevin had virtually been addicted to glam-rock, gleaning enormous musical inspiration from David Bowie, whom he had seen on the famous *Aladdin Sane* tour. 'Fachtna O'Ceallaigh promised that Morrissey would call me at home, but that never happened,' Nevin told me. 'I just sent him some tapes through the post and waited for his response, which seemed to take for ever. A few years before, I had formed Fairground Attraction with Eddi Reader. Soon afterwards we topped the charts with "Perfect".

Well, the group had since split up, and I suddenly received a postcard from Morrissey. It was the first of hundreds, and he had scrawled across it just one word – "PERFECT!" I was thrilled.'

Clive Langer then brought in Andrew Paresi, the drummer from *Viva Hate*, the former Madness bassist Mark 'Bedders' Bedford, and the Indian raga-violinist Nawazith Ali Khan. The line-up was completed by Seamus Behan and Steve Hart on keyboards – the latter, formerly the keyboard player for Elvis Costello and The Attractions, had also appeared on *The Jonathan Ross Show* as Steve Nieve (fronting the resident band, The Playboys), but according to contemporary reports Morrissey considered the name too ludicrous to be printed on an album cover, and it had to be changed. A few weeks later, a press statement was released by Clive Langer's manager, Jake Riviera, the man who as head of F-Beat Records had auditioned Johnny Marr's White Dice eleven years before. Part of this read: 'This is a really soulful Morrissey . . . his roots are free, he's telling a great story matched with a great piece of music.'

To whet the appetite, one of the tracks from the forthcoming *Kill Uncle* album was released as a single in February 1991. 'Our Frank', coupled with 'Journalists Who Lie' (a title reflecting the sentiments of many). ('Tony The Pony', the very first Morrissey-Nevin collaboration, was added to these for the 12-inch/CD.) 'Our Frank' is a gently cynical ballad which, surprisingly, only reached number 26 in the charts – surprising in that it is far removed from anything Morrissey had ever done with The Smiths, whose demise and possible reunion remained a constant interview topic until, almost savagely, the singer hit out with, 'I don't want to talk about The Smiths any more. Things are moving on. I've done well, and people should recognize that. Give it a rest, won't you?'

In future concert performances, the 'cigarette' line in 'Our Frank' often led to Morrissey being pelted with cigarettes from reformed smokers. On more than one occasion, when he sang the lines 'Give us a drink and make it quick/Or else I'm gonna be sick all over/Your frankly vulgar red pullover', such a garment was casually tossed on to the stage! But had Morrissey, in slightly amending his style, become a 'reformed' character? Reformed, that is, of his so-called, much-publicized misery? This particular question brought the response: 'Underneath this shell there's a raging skinhead trying to get out!'

The most important of these self-effected changes came about with Morrissey's constant angst, since turning solo, of having no backing musicians which were exclusively his. Although he had worked well with Mark Nevin, the guitarist had contractual obligations elsewhere which prevented him from going on the road, and the fans were of course anxious to see Morrissey, bearing in mind the almost peevish lack of airplay which continued to plague him. The singer therefore engaged four versatile young men who, in a Britain ravaged by recession, had probably spent more time looking for work than actually doing any.

The first to be summoned to the Morrissey court was a 27-year-old guitarist named Boz Boorer, who had worked with Sinead O'Connor and several minor groups. In 1978, Boorer had joined The Polecats, described as 'a genuine rockabilly band', an outfit whose average age had been just fifteen. They had released several singles on the Nervous label, including 'Rockabilly Rebel/Chicken Shack', which Morrissey is said to have liked, and an album for Phonogram. They had also played extensively in Europe and New York, before folding at the end of 1990, ironically coinciding with Boorer's meeting with his future mentor at a Holland Park restaurant. Whilst mulling over Morrissey's very attractive offer, Boorer had augmented the re-formed John's Children, whose original guitarist had been none other than Marc Bolan. Morrissey's pulling power, however, proved irresistible.

Another short-lived rockabilly outfit which greatly impressed Morrissey was The Memphis Sinners, comprising Alain Whyte and Spencer Cobrin – respectively lead guitar/backing vocals and the drummer from the defunct Born Bad – and the omni-tattooed fifties rock and roll enthusiast, Gary Day. All were in their early to mid-twenties, and the quartet were invited by Morrissey to appear in the promotional film for 'Sing Your Life', after which they were engaged full-time.

What is remarkable, perhaps, is that neither Whyte nor Cobrin had been ardent Smiths fans. The former counted this a good point, saying, 'This is one of the reasons we've got on so well with Mozz. The fact that he was in The Smiths doesn't mean a lot to us. We've taken him for what he is – a good bloke. As a band, we get on well.' Spencer Cobrin, who had been raised on a diet of Led Zepplin, The Kinks, Jimi Hendrix and The Who, was more to the point, confessing, 'It was the sort of music that, if it came on the radio, I'd turn it off.' By far the shortest of the ensemble, Cobrin more than compensated for any lack of stature with his muscular, ferocious drumming style, comparable with and almost rivalling that of Mike Joyce. As he himself put it when a concerned American fan commented on the callouses on his hands, 'Balls-out is my only speed!'

Morrissey's new regime coincided with the release of his new album, *Kill Uncle*, during the spring of 1991. The singer was now about to enter his 'black phase' with the British music press, a period where there were times when every single move he made seemed to be met with journalistic scorn and disapproval – even the simple question, 'Who was the singer with The Smiths?' posed on a television quiz-show earned a sarcastic paragraph in one publication. Mark Nevin said to me, 'I remember asking myself, why did these people have to be so ugly? It just shows how wicked some people can be when you give them a pen and an opportunity to write something in a newspaper. That's why I feel

Morrissey enjoys touring so much. Because of the way the press in this country has turned against him, he likes to be where he's more appreciated, like in America where they're more positive about him. The British press live in this journalists' Never-Never World where people do all these weird things that only make sense in a newspaper.'

Even Tony Parsons, the respected pop journalist who later championed Morrissey's cause by attacking his severest critics, could not resist taking a dig at him in the *Independent*.

He's the embodiment of the pimply angst that seethes behind polite lace curtains. He is a music-hall Hamlet, a stand-up depressive . . . but, three solo albums down the line, the patron saint of miserable little buggers is still waiting for solo greatness to come along. There is a fair bit to bill and coo over here, but it lacks the wild beauty of Mr Mozza's glory days with Johnny Marr and The Smiths. Let's hope he hasn't lost Johnny Marr's number.

Morrissey hit out vehemently at such criticism, and at his fans' now tedious lamenting for The Smiths, in an interview with Stuart Maconie of the *New Musical Express* – the very last time he afforded the publication the time of day.

At the moment I look upon The Smiths as a dead cat that must be buried in a shoebox at the bottom of the garden. My past is almost denying me a future . . . as for The Smiths, I have my tin hat on, and I'm bringing down the blackout. This will seem an unreadably bloated remark but, as time goes by, my individuality is confirmed by those writers who can't stand my guts. They are constantly handing me back-handed compliments . . . I must mean more to them than their own mothers, and in their endless, poetic hatred of me, they have made me important. Of course, if I was truly in decline, no one would write a word about me!

1 'Celebrity is a form of revenge . . . but what else do I have to offer?'

2 'I am human and I want to be loved...'

3 'I am medicine ... and poison!'

4 'I am ready for that fiery furnace . . . there's not enough room in heaven for everyone!'

5 'Naked males should be splashed around the Co-op, you know!'

6 'Being English inspires me in a poetic way.'

7 'I'm incapable of putting on airs and graces for the sake of "the industry". I'm only capable of being myself.'

8 'I don't get any degree of support in America from the media . . . therefore my success, what I've achieved, is completely pure. There's no hype involved.'

9 'I have absolutely no desire to play Hamlet.'

10 'I don't think people consider me to be a superstar . . . I'm
just considered to be a British
phenomenon, as well as a sex
symbol.'

11 'It's so much easier to love
myths and legends . . . they never
answer back or deceive. And I've
always had such good taste!'

12 'My reputation goes before me and I can only follow . . . and
no matter what people say, I've won.'

13 'I want to be pinned on everybody's wall . . .'

14 'There's always a danger in trying to give an audience what it wants. I think it's more interesting to give an audience something it might not want.'

15-18   'One only has to listen to the tone of my voice, when I sing,
to realize that I exude no contempt, just love.'

19-22 'I'm not ready to go home . . . yet!'

 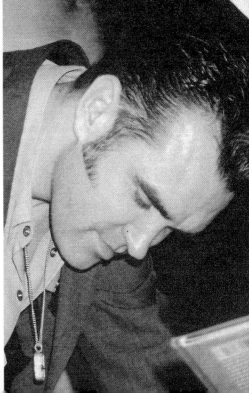

23 'I say things that are important . . . therefore I want fame.'

Kill Uncle shot into the album charts, peaking at number 8, and if there was any criticism from those all-important fans, it was that, at ten songs and 33 minutes, the piece was probably a little on the short side. Even so, it is a fine monument to Morrissey's songwriting skills and Mark Nevin's very personal musical intelligence – an album which is best savoured when the lights are dimmed and the listener is in a receptive, mellow mood.

Kill Uncle opens with the already familiar 'Our Frank', running directly into 'Asian Rut', a bittersweet song performed with great feeling and compassion, in which Morrissey's anguish over his subject's unwarranted predicament becomes a baying lament, each tormented phrase accentuated by the strains of the raga-violin. Incredibly, sections of the media actually accused Morrissey of racism, and the *New Musical Express* found him guilty of 'playing games, gently stoking the fires, dodging behind words and trying to get up noses'. This was of course utter piffle, for the objective of the song was the exact opposite. A few months later, Morrissey lashed out at these ridiculous slurs, stating quite categorically, 'I'm incapable of racism, even though an increasing number of my audience are skinheads in nail-varnish. The people who say I'm racist are basically just the people who can't stand the sight of my physical frame – I don't think we should flatter them with our attention.'

'The first time I heard Morrissey speak the lyrics aloud, I came close to tears,' Mark Nevin enthused. 'And how can anyone call the song racist when it's so blatantly *anti*-racist? Does that mean that you aren't allowed to mention Asian people without being called racist? I thought it the best song on *Kill Uncle*, just as "Bengali in Platforms" was my favourite song on *Viva Hate*. When I first heard *that* song – well, words can't express its brilliance. Life really *is* hard when you don't belong here! And what you said is right. Morrissey *does* climb into the other person's skin.

"November Spawned a Monster" is another superb example of that.'

A 'tooled-up' Asian boy has arrived, seeking retribution for the murder of his only friend in a three-against-one attack by English thugs, though even the eyewitness narrator is unsure of the eventual outcome of the confrontation when the brakes fail and the gun jams.

The third song on the album, 'Sing Your Life', was released as a single in March 1991, and stalled at number 33 in the hit-parade in spite of being coupled with the excellent 'The Loop' and Paul Weller's 'That's Entertainment'. 'Mute Witness', one of the two poems on the album set to Clive Langer's music, once again tackles the tricky subject of disablement – in this instance the difficulties experienced by a deaf and dumb girl who is desperately trying to describe something which has distressed her.

The other Langer collaboration was 'Found, Found, Found', an ode to Morrissey's close friendship with Michael Stipe, the gifted, frail-looking singer from the American group R E M. Stipe, then aged 30 and as renowned for his intense privacy and almost point-blank refusal to speak about himself as for his lachrymose vocal technique, had been writing to Morrissey for some time, and initially the slightly older Mancunian had not known quite what to make of this. Eventually, he had agreed to a private meeting during which the pair 'walked in huge circles through Hyde Park', as had happened during his formative years with Linder. 'Found, found, found – someone who's worth it in this murkiness,' Morrissey proclaims to the heavy pounding of the drums, interspersed with sparse, well-chosen fragments of dialogue.

Morrissey told the press, 'Michael is a very generous, kind person. The whole joy about the friendship is that music doesn't ever come into it. We don't ever talk about R E M or whatever it is I do. There are other things to discuss . . . and who knows, we may even get a cover on *Hello!*' He was referring to the time-honoured superstition that 'couples' who appear on the cover of the famous glossy gossip weekly usually find that their relationship flounders soon after – said with tongue firmly in cheek, of course. Such reservations aside, he was not entirely negative when asked if the pair would ever work together. He said to Mark Kemp of *Select*, 'It would be nice to do something unusual, some Righteous Brothers type thing. I'd like to lead the way. It could be one of those funny, historic bits of television that's so rare these days, especially in England.'

The wistful 'Driving your Girlfriend Home', with Linder on backing vocals, presents Morrissey as a kindly 'agony uncle' who is explaining to a friend's boyfriend the despondency in the relationship she is trying hard to avoid. He tells him, 'She's laughing to stop herself crying'. The plight of the long-suffering girlfriend resurfaces in 'King Leer', when comfort is forthcoming from 'vodka and Tizer', 'a homeless chihuahua', and the narrator offering himself physically – though any act of love is largely uneventful, and the singer's concern is recompensed only with abject ingratitude.

In 'The Harsh Truth of the Camera Eye', the storyteller is the photographer who shares the humiliation of his subject's compulsion to put on an act in public life, and his/her avid reluctance to face the press. There is also a neat touch of the autobiographical in the closing lines: 'I don't want to be judged/I would sooner be just blindly loved.' And, of course, with 'The Last of the Family Line' there is the customary donning of the hair-shirt for, after fifteen generations of 'honouring nature', the narrator's family are presented with a throw-back, though even here there is some solace – Morrissey, as the last survivor, is thankfully 'spared the pain of ever saying goodbye'.

The closing song on the album is 'There's a Place in Hell for Me and My Friends', and the truly dazzling studio-version of this, wonderfully enriched by Mark Nevin's solitary piano accompaniment (more poignant than Morrissey's later live renditions of the song) becomes a graceful hymn to malignity and could almost be the singer writing his own epitaph . . . the fact that death, in common with nakedness, enables all manner of mankind to become equal.

Morrissey's predilection for outmoded imagery, as displayed by his choice of sleeves for The Smiths' recordings, enabled him to set another precedent for his forthcoming *Kill Uncle* tour when he announced that his 'mascot' would be the English poet Edith Sitwell (1887–1964), who once maintained that she had acquired her immense wisdom from a lengthy, unrequited love affair with the Russian painter Pavel Tchelitchew – unrequited because of his homosexuality.

The Sitwells – Edith and her two equally famous younger brothers named Osbert and Sacheverell – were in some ways the Warhols of their day, possessed of an urbane charm, patrician values, and a passion for culture which had yielded a veritable stream of essays and poems covering almost every aspect of architecture, painting, music, and life itself. The American drama critic, James Agate, had called them 'artists pretending to be asses', Noël Coward had used them as a basis for his parody of 1923, 'Swiss Family Whittlebot' (in '*London Calling*'), and Sitwell herself pontificated at one of her world-famous Bayswater tea-parties, 'I have been brought up on Rhythm as other children are brought up on Glaxo!', a statement which probably tickled Morrissey's ribs when he selected the photograph which would embellish tour posters, backstage passes, laminates, and a backdrop which his fans would find very amusing.

Like Morrissey, Edith Sitwell had nurtured a fondness for hats, though unlike him her varied assortment of creations – pompadours, turbans, plumes and even stuffed birds – rarely suited her heavy-lidded, bony features. When she had sailed to New York in 1948, draped from head to toe in black Florentine brocade – 'in mourning for the world' – she had run into Cecil Beaton, the photographer whose portrait of Truman Capote graced The Smiths' 'The Boy With the

Thorn in his Side'. Beaton snapped her in profile, looking bird-like in a high toque, clasping her multi-ringed, lizardous hands to her breast. It was by no means the most unusual photograph of Sitwell ever taken, but against the stage back-drop it was the most impressive.

In fact, due to a last-minute technicians' hitch, the Sitwell backdrop was conspicuous by its absence at the Dublin National Stadium on 27 April 1991, the first venue of Morrissey's tour. The two thousand tickets had all been sold within one hour of the shutters going up at the ascribed HMV office – hundreds of fans had camped overnight in the street to be sure of access to the standing-area in front of the stage – the announcement had gone out already that the low podium would have no protection barrier, thus promising a maximum of body-hugging invasions, as essential to Morrissey as the flowers his fans clutched. Phranc, the off-beat American folk-singer, braved a support-slot which forty minutes later was described by one onlooker as 'a tableau of adoration', before the house lights dipped to an overture comprising David Bowie's 'Laughing Gnome' to an aria from the German neo-operatic gender-bender Klaus Nomi. Born Klaus Spender in 1942, his name was an anagram of the cyberpunk sci-fi magazine, *Omni*. Morrissey had first seen him on *The Old Grey Whistle Test* in 1980, since which time he had backed David Bowie, played a Rhine maiden in Wagner's *Ring* Cycle, and recorded two best-selling albums. The strangest looking of all the glam-rock stars, Nomi often appeared on stage wearing outfits which looked as though they had come straight out of *Blake's Seven*, garish make-up, and a tri-peaked hairstyle. Flagrantly homosexual, he died in 1983 and was one of the first showbusiness celebrities to die of AIDS. Until being 'revived' by Morrissey, he had been almost forgotten.

The venue was in fact a boxing stadium and, this in mind, Stuart Maconie reported in the *New Musical Express*, 'Rabbit-punched by his former friends, declared out for the count by a score of Harry Carpenters, the old champ is coaxed out of retirement for another shot at the crown.' To a myriad popping flashbulbs and deafening applause, Morrissey made a stupendous entrance and stood stock-still for fully two minutes, arms outstretched like a hero returned from the front, having swapped his trenchcoat for close-fitting Levi's and a baggy gold lurex chemise. Those fans expecting to get close to their idol, however, were shocked to find their 'patch' set out with seats – mindless of the security, and risking the wrath of the Garda, these were passed hand-to-hand to the back of the auditorium, whence the crowd were able to surge forwards, pelting Morrissey with thousands of flowers.

Morrissey's opening number, 'Interesting Drug', was virtually inaudible on account of the excitement. Afterwards, an admirer somehow got hold of a microphone to yell, 'I love you, Steven!' – to which he responded, 'Thank you, but I don't know who Steven is!' During 'Mute Witness', the stage invasions tottered on the brink of danger and he found himself gently rebuking, 'This is all very touching, but if you stay *off* the stage we'll be able to play *better*!' Minor hysteria prevailed during the next few songs, but when Morrissey doubled up 'in agony' during 'November Spawned a Monster', it was too much for some, and parts of the audience were genuinely alarmed until he suddenly sprang to his feet. A fierce rugby-tackle brought him down during 'Our Frank' and he hit the floor with a terrific thud, though the carpet of mushy flowers helped to cushion the blow – looking up, he sang with a growl the appropriate line, '*give it a rest, won't you?*', and this earned him a mighty roar of approval.

Several songs were given their première in Dublin, including 'Pregnant for the Last Time' and the delectable 'I've Changed My Plea to Guilty', by which time Morrissey had changed into a shredded black shirt which would not survive the evening. The New York Dolls' 'Trash', a late addition to his set, was introduced as a tribute to Johnny Thunders, who had died only a few days before. For many, however, the song which gave them a real 'buzz' was Morrissey's and Alain Whyte's mindblowing version of Paul Weller's retaliatory song, 'That's Entertainment', described by one eyewitness as 'orgasmic'. The song was an acerbic response to the Irving Berlin song of the same name, crooned in the 1950s by Judy Garland and Ethel Merman, though the Weller interpretation of entertainment culminated only with 'Blood-spattered walls' and 'a kick in the balls'.

The reviews for Morrissey's Dublin concert – his first full-length performance in Great Britain in more than four years – were ecstatic. Michael Bracewell of the *Guardian* paraphrased Oscar Wilde: 'He has nothing to declare but his genius.' Even the pseudonymous Everett True, reporting indignantly and at times rudely for the *Melody Maker*, could not resist summing him up as 'The most charismatic performer this side of an Oliver Stone movie'. And Cathy Dillon of *Hot Press*, who spoke to a perspiring, bare-chested Morrissey immediately after the event, proclaimed him 'An interviewer's dream – Woody Allen's mind in Montgomery Clift's body.' To prove the latter point, if proof was indeed required, the photograph accompanying Dillon's lament for Smithdom – airbrushed and cleverly shaded below the waist – may have actually been intended to give the impression that the subject had posed naked, which of course he had not.

Two days after Dublin, Morrissey played the Élysée Montmartre, in Paris. The performance was taped by Bernard Lemoin of France-Inter Radio's *Pop-Club*, and relayed later in the week. Several years on, it appeared as a bootleg CD, *Posing in Paris*. Although Morrissey was an infrequent visitor to the French capital and not familiar with the language, the people had taken him to their hearts. One journalist had compared him with Barbara, the greatest of all the modern French popular singers since Piaf – a comparison which is neither condescending nor bizarre. Barbara, born in 1930, has been conducting an intensely private love affair with her audiences for almost 40 years, enjoying concert seasons, tours, and chart-topping albums divided by lengthy, almost crippling periods of solitude where all is shunned for the confines of her country retreat. And, as with Morrissey, Barbara's lyrics have centred on several of those subjects frowned upon by the Anglo-Saxon world – her first big hit in Europe, 'Nantes', tells of the death and roadside burial of her errant father. Like Morrissey, Barbara has always placed the love of her public before the love of any partner in particular. Like Morrissey, her best work has invariably been in front of an audience.

These comparisons and qualities were not overlooked by Jean-Daniel Beauvallet of France's most prestigious popular music magazine, *Les Inrockuptibles*, who asked Morrissey if he was at all frightened of the prospect of growing old alone. Had such a pertinent question been posed by a potentially sarcastic or tongue-in-cheek British reporter, the response might have been equally flippant. In effect, it was rather sad.

Whatever happens to me now, my situation could never be as bad as when I was sixteen. Do you remember the poem 'At Seventeen', by Janis Ian? At seventeen I learned that love is only reserved for the winners of beauty contests. I could say that having money makes life easier the older one gets . . . the truth is, as I get older I'm better able to understand myself and tame my terrible depressions. I can't eliminate them entirely, though I have learned to confront them head-on. When you've endured such an atrocious childhood, you've to make the best of what's left. The only certain companion for me is myself, though I've always waited for the right person to come banging on my door . . . the only way I have of escaping from my own particular world is by letting someone else in. She never comes, so I have to make do with my dreams.

Kill Uncle was named Album of the Year by the French music press. *Les Inrockuptibles* enthused: 'Uncle Momo has buried his past, and now looks towards heaven during his second solo stop on his march towards glory.' His most requested song in France was 'There's a Place in Hell for Me and My Friends', and when asked if he merited such a place, he replied quite seriously, 'There's no other alternative. Some of us *have* to end up down there, and I'm ready to suffer the flames. In any case, there won't be enough room in heaven for us all.' At the end of 1993, I myself adapted the song into French, entitling it, 'Y'a un p'tit coin privé'.

After his concerts in Dienze and Utrecht, Morrissey moved on to Germany. His entourage had been augmented by Stuart Maconie, again working for the *New Musical Express*. Maconie, a friendly individual with an unmistakable Lancastrian twang which must have been a great comfort to the singer in foreign climes, and who abhorred the shabby, prejudiced treatment Morrissey was getting from some quarters, was invited to partake of the evening revelries. He told me, 'Morrissey was in his element in Berlin, laughing all the time and cracking jokes. He's a very witty man. Somebody wanted him to pose for a photograph, so he lay down in the middle of the road and got hit by a bicycle. He just stood up and said, "I don't know whether to throw the bike into the Rhine, or whatever the river's called here, or act like a perfect gentleman, which is something I'm good at!" Later on myself, Morrissey, the lads from the band and a few others had a couple of drinks in the hotel bar, and I suggested going walkabout. That surprised him a bit, being treated like a mate. So we set off around Berlin looking for things to do. We went into a couple of clubs, but none of them were brilliant, so we all talked. He told me that he was frighteningly happy, and he seemed to enjoy being treated like a normal person, which is what he is. I'm telling you this because I'm from Wigan, and

Morrissey's at his most relaxed when he's with other Northerners. I'm also very proud that one of the best interviews he ever did was with me. Us Northerners have to stick together!'

What made Maconie's interview with Morrissey truly inspiring – his best British one since the one with Paul Morley, and to date unsurpassed – was the absolute absence of misinterpretation. The singer's comments were published verbatim, and the journalist did not attempt to draw attention to himself at the expense of his subject. Morrissey was lionized as 'an enormous, capricious talent who's come through a hail of slings and arrows of outrageous fortune with the stoic optimism of Captain Mainwaring.' And at a time when the tabloids were into their 'outing' phase, the headline MORRISSEY COMES OUT! (FOR A DRINK) was in itself an attack on the system. And, as to be expected, Morrissey's views were rich with gritty humour.

On the subject of idolatry: 'At the risk of sounding more pompous than I am, I always was more loved than admired. Eric Clapton may be *admired* but who would *love* him? His mother, perhaps?' On the subject of his success: 'Everything I've worked for over these last twenty-four months has gone right. At the core of that are the four individuals I'm working with. People should realize that now instead of in the year 2001. I don't want people to wait until I've been hit by a milkfloat to realize what a great group this is.' On his despondency with the current music scene: 'You're kidding if you think The Manic Street Preachers mean anything to anyone. Watching *Top of the Pops* and, I shudder to say it, MTV, is like watching a road accident.' Most important of all, on patriotism: 'Skinheads in nail varnish represent the Britain I love. The skinhead was an entirely British invention. If ever I was asked for an autograph by someone wearing some of those awful Cure baseball boots, I'd take it as a sign from hell that the curtain was coming down!'

Morrissey was also asked the hypothetical question (in

view of Everett True's observation after the Dublin concert) who he thought should play him when Oliver Stone got around to the film. He replied, 'Well, I think it ought to be Dirk Bogarde. I mean, Dandy Nichols is dead, isn't she?'

Tim Broad took advantage of the sojourn in Berlin, completing the promotional film for Morrissey's next single, 'Pregnant for the Last Time'. He and the band were seen visiting the famous Brandenburg Gate, performing on stage at the Metropol Theatre, and playing frisbee with Morrissey's tambourine. There was an impromptu appearance by Eva Busch, the veteran actress-singer who had been Marlene Dietrich's rival during the days of the Weimar Republic, and the outrageous glam-rock star Jobriath (of whom more later) was seen on an album cover brandished by Morrissey. And of course there was the now obligatory flaunting of flesh to reveal what Morrissey had written across his chest – first the word SINGER, then the word VOICE, in capital letters – a far cry from the INITIATE ME slogan that he had scrawled over his middle for a photograph which had once appeared on the cover of the *New Musical Express* and which, during the German visit, ended up on a bootleg poster.

The brief but exhausting European tour ended a few days later in Copenhagen, leaving a seven-day gap before Morrissey's three concerts in Scotland. In Aberdeen on 14 May he complained of feeling unwell. A severe throat infection was diagnosed, but the show went ahead as planned. His throat finally gave up on him the next evening when, after the ninth song, he was forced to leave the stage at Dundee's Caird Hall. This time there was no question of his continuing – his doctor ordered him to cancel the next day's concert at the prestigious Glasgow Concert Hall. The move caused pandemonium amongst fans, who were eventually placated by a statement that Morrissey would return to Glasgow immediately after his American tour, scheduled to begin at the San Diego Sports Arena on 30 May.

There was also talk of Morrissey and his support-act,

Phranc, recording an updated version of the 1975 Elton John-Kiki Dee chart-topper, 'Don't Go Breaking My Heart'. The singer is said to have issued a statement condemning the 'doom and gloom' of pop music, adding, 'Our song will help break the ice at discos and stop the boys huddling together in corners and make them ask the girls to go for a twirl around the tiles.' Like several other 'proposed' duets, this seems to have had little or no substance, and was almost certainly an attempt by the music press to discredit the singer – the fact that if Morrissey could be 'proved' to be unprofessional, unethical and belligerent by cancelling arrangements which had probably never been made in the first place, then his fans would lose faith and desert him. Exactly why some journalists treated him with such odious contempt, and still do, cannot be readily explained, for no matter what they said about Morrissey, the fans stuck like glue and no doubt will continue to do so. As for his alleged pairing with Phranc, who left the tour at the end of May because of a family bereavement, he dismissed this in a contemporaneous interview with Mark Kemp of *Select*, saying, 'I could never ever begin to explain the utter loathing I feel for dance music. That two people can sit in their bedroom in Detroit with a little bit of machinery and come out with this huge wall of sound is sterility at its utmost. I want to see *real* people on stage, playing *real* instruments.'

On a more serious note, Kemp asked Morrissey what he would do if it all ended suddenly. The singer replied, almost with abject indifference, 'I'd live in a crumbling cottage in Somerset. I wouldn't try to claw my way back.'

8

But Please Hold That Sunrise Below . . .

If American ticket-sales were anything to go by, Morrissey's rural retreat was a long way off. Of the 27 venues proposed for the first leg of the *Kill Uncle* tour, most had sold out in record time – the 20,000-seater San Diego Sports Arena in less than an hour, and the 14,000 tickets for the Los Angeles Forum had gone at the rate of 1,000 per minute. These figures are all the more astonishing when one considers that Morrissey had still not enjoyed actual chart success in America, whilst British bands who had – such as Jesus Jones and EMF – were experiencing considerable difficulty filling 3,000-seater provincial halls. Only the Sacramento Exposition Center proved disappointing, with 60 per cent of the 13,000 tickets remaining unsold due to allegedly poor advertising. Such was the demand for tickets at some venues that groups of disappointed fans could be seen waving Edith Sitwell posters at freeway exits, flagging down similarly recognizable fans with $100 bills!

Morrissey was inundated with requests to give interviews. Not surprisingly, he turned them all down, though he did allow the cameras to follow him into the Orange County Pacific Ampitheatre on 1 June to film a sound-check. Wearing a black coat, Sitwell T-shirt and pass, dark glasses and a large hat, he ran through 'Sing Your Life'. His career was also the subject of a local television programme, *Request Video*, hosted by Gia Desautis, who was allowed to speak with the band and reacted giddily, asking several silly questions including, 'What is the funniest thing Morrissey's done whilst he's been here?' Most of the musicians' replies were monosyllabic, and Spencer Cobrin seemed positively bored and at one stage appeared to fall asleep.

The American fans, too, were quite different from their clonish British counterparts – according to one observer, at one concert they consisted of 'androgynous teenagers, Latino gangsters and booted skinheads, suited thirtysome-things, a few stray gays, and a handful of senior citizens.' Jo Slee, Morrissey's personal assistant and his manager in all but name, told reporters at a press conference, 'He attracts this gentle adoration from everybody, but you'd need a degree in sociology to work him out.'

These American admirers, initially at least, were not given the opportunity to whip up much enthusiasm, which must have been extremely frustrating when one considers the fire and passion which Morrissey injected into each perfor-mance. At Berkeley on 8 June the audience was instructed to remain seated during the concert and 'missiles' – in other words, flowers – were strictly prohibited. To appease the generosity of his fans, large cardboard boxes were posi-tioned at the entrance to the Greek Theatre, marked 'GIFTS FOR MORRISSEY', and these were rapidly piled high with cards, packages, flowers, superfluous volumes of Oscar Wilde, and, for reasons unknown, dozens of packets of pork scratchings! Morrissey, suitably attired for the occasion in jeans, white shirt and blazer, strolled on to the stage and announced, 'Good evening . . . San Francisco!'

In Phoenix on 11 June, the promotional film was made for 'My Love Life', though at the time no actual plans had been made to release it as a single – in Britain, EMI were about to release 'Pregnant for the Last Time'. The film, throughout which Morrissey was seen driving his band through the streets of the city in a hired limousine, was effectively shot in black and white and reminiscent of David Lynch, even more so with the dreamy musical introduction.

Morrissey's concert at the Dallas Starplex on 17 June was filmed in its entirety, also by Tim Broad, and 'put in storage' for future release as a commercial video – not Morrissey's best performance vocally, though most of the faults in the finished copy were unavoidable technical ones. It was also one of his first shows, though by no means the last, to end prematurely because of a stage invasion – albeit in the sixteenth song – a problem no doubt exacerbated by over-excitement following a guitar-smashing sequence after 'That's Entertainment'. Unfairly, other fans found themselves penalized for this later in the tour; 12,000 fans who turned up for the concert in Detroit were warned of the 'perils' of crossing the barrier, though this did not deter three youngsters, one of whom reached up and placed an expensive gold pendant about Morrissey's neck and the other two being *invited* by him to sing backing vocals on 'Sing your Life'. The singer watched helplessly as all three were dragged into the wings by bouncers, handed over to armed police, and subsequently fined $35 for 'civil violation'.

On 25 June, Morrissey played to one of his biggest audiences ever when 30,000 fans crammed into Chicago's World Theater – many of whom had hardly ever heard him on mainstream radio. In an interview with Greg Kot of the *Chicago Tribune*, the singer accused the executives at Sire, his American record company, of feeding radio stations with rumours of his alleged awkwardness, adding, 'It's disheartening, but I would never, to coin that delightful American expression, kiss ass. I don't want to become a commodity, a dishrag.' He also declared that, for him, the precognitive dream still held fast, telling Kot, 'I'm completely fatalistic in that I believe whatever happens is meant to happen for the eventual good, if not the immediate good. Though I can go through moments that are quite depressing, I secretly know that I'll profit from them. I just have to wait and see *why* things happen.'

Morrissey's American tour culminated in a superb concert on 13 July at New York's Madison Square Garden, after which he was felicitated by old friends Lloyd Cole and Michael Stipe.

His first London show in five years, one week later at Wembley Arena, was preceded by chaos when trains to the venue were terminated several miles from their destination. Whilst unaware of this, Morrissey inadvertently made matters worse by bringing the show forward by thirty minutes, resulting in one mad dash for all, with many fans missing the support slot altogether (Phranc had returned for the seven British dates) and the first few songs. Thus, much of the effect anticipated by the curtains opening on the huge Tom Courtenay backdrop was lost.

In the heat of the moment, the microphone failed during the first song, 'Interesting Drug' – a point naturally picked up by the music press, whose headlines 'MORRISSEY DELIVERS: IT'S A BOY!' and 'FROM HERE TO MATERNITY!' were allusions to his new single, 'Pregnant for the Last Time', whose uniquely North-of-England lyrics had probably been lost on most of his American fans.

The reviews in the British music press were vacuous, offensive, and often lacking in taste and professional integrity. The *New Musical Express*'s saving grace was a sensational collection of action shots by Kevin Cummins. One, showing the singer draped upside-down over a monitor, remains definitive. The politely serious critics from the broadsheets, on the other hand, were appreciative though they did agree almost unanimously that several songs were marred by the frantic dashing back and forth of the musicians, mindlessly so during tender numbers like 'Asian Rut'. David Sinclair of *The Times*, who praised Morrissey's singing as 'a model of unfussy conviction', called it 'one of the most gripping spectacles likely to be seen this year'. Morrissey, on the other hand, was excused his 'eccentricities', such as prostrating himself before a fan, staring fixedly into the young man's eyes and pronouncing, 'Why do *you* come here?' – or by performing most of 'Mute Witness' on his back, feet pointing towards the rafters and executing, according to *Select*, 'a mating ritual originally meant for some species of parrot'. There was also the moment when a burly fan clambered on to the stage and attempted what seemed like a potentially dangerous bear-hug from behind – only to find himself raised bodily, inches from the ground, and swung around in such a way that those nearest the stage actually ducked! As Linder Sterling told me, 'So many people underestimate Morrissey. They don't even begin to realize how phenomenally strong he is!'

Morrissey remained in the capital one more night to play the Brixton Academy, before moving on to Brighton, Liverpool, Doncaster, Blackpool, and the Royal Concert Hall in Glasgow, where fans were still lamenting the May cancellation. Here, some of the bouncers were more thuggish thán they had been in America. There were reports of them handing out paper cups of water to parched fans prior to the performance, only to knock around anyone who attempted to get on to the stage during the show.

The announcement of Morrissey's impending visit to Japan was of sufficient importance to make the front page of the staid, usually anti-showbusiness *Nihon Keizai Shinbun*, the country's equivalent of the *Financial Times*, on 23 August 1991. Four days later he played his first concert at the recently built Fukuoka Sun Palace, a relatively small venue where security was overtly heavy-handed. For reasons known only to themselves, the Japanese authorities brought forward the starting times of Morrissey's concerts, the Sun Palace one by two hours. Not only were fans searched on their way into the building, they were requested to hand over their flowers – these were examined for hidden devices and drugs, labelled, and passed on to the singer. Additionally, an official police warning was issued against stage invasions, though this was ignored when a large section of the audience surged forwards and an over-enthusiastic handshake resulted in Morrissey having a shirt-sleeve ripped off. This of course did not bother him in the least, but the actions of

these youngsters, perfectly acceptable elsewhere in the
world, would have severe repercussions later in the week.

Preferring not to stay in a Fukuoka Hotel, Morrissey and
his entourage boarded the bullet-train to Osaka only hours
after the show – followed by two dozen admirers, including
a young lady named Kanako Ishikawa who, through her
sheer politeness, quickly earned Morrissey's respect, and
who later founded the excellent *Lucky Lisp* fanzine. Though
very tired, the singer was patient with the handful of
Kanako's friends who managed to bypass the still-persistent
security and enter his carriage, signing autographs and chat-
ting amicably. These Japanese fans were considerably more
fortunate than their peers, for Morrissey had flatly refused to
give press interviews or meet officials from EMI-Toshiba.
The company had recently issued a Japan-only 6-track CD,
and one of the songs, 'That's Entertainment', had been subsequently banned by some radio stations for allegedly inciting eruptions between fans and bouncers.

In Osaka the directors of the 8,000-seater County Hall
took very seriously the rumours of an impending riot, and
ordered barriers to be installed not just around the stage
area, but in the gangways. The actual concert, said to be
Morrissey's finest in Japan, was professionally recorded but
only issued as a bootleg CD, *Nothing to Declare But My
Jeans*.

On 1 September at the Nagoya Century Hall, another
small new building, a scuffle broke out after fans had pelted
Morrissey with hundreds of cigarettes during 'Our Frank'.
Dissension came to a head the next day in Tokyo, when
10,000 fans flocked to the famous Budokan to find that each
block of seats had been enclosed by a tall, fence-like struc-
ture. 'Morrissey spent part of the morning walking around
the animal market,' Kanako said bitterly. 'That evening, *we*
were the ones in cages. It was such a cold, horrible atmosphere to be in.' Worse than this, several fans whose only
'crime' had been to get out of their seats, were dragged

bodily from the arena and ejected into the street.

Tokyo, thankfully, did have its lighter, even amusing moments. During a record-buying walkabout, Morrissey suddenly found himself surrounded by dozens of out-of-town tourists who snapped away happily for almost an hour – before asking members of his entourage *who* they had photographed! A handful of older fans, witness to the glam-rock explosion of the early seventies, began making on the face of it grossly unfair comparisons between Morrissey and one of the era's more colourful and controversial figures. Such comparisons were escalated by the singer himself, however, when he began handing out scraps of paper inscribed, 'MISTAKEN FOR JOBRIATH YET AGAIN!' and confessed that he had been a fan of the star who was allegedly the inspiration behind the Marc Bolan song, 'Cosmic Dancer', one of the B-sides on the *Pregnant for the Last Time* CD which had been recorded on stage in Utrecht.

Jobriath Boone, born around 1945, had launched himself on the New York underground music-scene in 1972 when, claiming to have signed a $½ million with Elektra, he commissioned a nude poster of himself, measuring 41 × 43 feet, to be pasted on a hoarding in Times Square. This was observed by a French impresario, who made immediate comparisons with the infamous Texan man-woman, Van der Clyde, who had visited Paris in 1925, met Jean Cocteau and changed his name to Barbette. Appearing in a nude revue at the Folies-Bergère, he had executed a perilous tightrope routine in blonde wig and dress – removing the former to reveal a totally bald head, and the latter to reveal that he was a man! At the Paris Opera House in 1973, Jobriath had promoted his début album and the curtain had opened on him dressed as King Kong, 'mounting' a 50-foot phallus-shaped Empire State Building! Morrissey's admiration for this singer had resulted in a cameo appearance of the album cover in the Berlin video, and it also appeared on the cover of the Japanese CD. He also enthused over the way Jobriath had withdrawn from show business, vanishing without trace in 1975 shortly after releasing his second album, *Creatures of the Street*.

In fact, Jobriath had not disappeared at all. Failing magnificently in his attempt to become the world's first openly gay superstar, he had retreated to a life of drugs and debauchery at London's then infamous Chelsea Hotel, famed for being one of the cherished haunts of the Warhol clan, and even more so for its 'celebrity suicides'. Nancy Spungen, Sid Vicious and the drag queen Christina had all expired there, and in 1985 Jobriath was taken from his tawdry room to a local hospital, where he died of an AIDs-related illness. His last words are alleged to have been, 'Please hold that sunrise below, if you don't mind.'

Morrissey's final concert in Japan was at the massive 15,000-seater Yokohama Arena. Again, problems were caused by bullying bouncers, so much so that at one point the singer smashed his microphone against one of the barriers. The next morning he took the train to Narita airport, and many of the fans who turned up to wish him bon voyage admitted that they would not have been in the least surprised had he announced that he would never visit the country again. He did not, though suffice to say the people of Japan are still waiting.

A year or so later, in Morrissey's 'honour', a Japanese publishing house, thinking they were acting in his fans' interests, attempted to right several wrongs by releasing a volume of his lyrics in translation. An impressive-looking tome of 335 pages, it was the brainchild of folksinger-journalist Goroh Nakagawa, and comprised all 112 Smiths songs, and some 90 per cent of Morrissey's – 'Piccadilly Palare' and several other vernacular numbers were given up as a bad job. The Japanese rendition of 'This Charming Man' was a real stinker, suddenly becoming an ode to male prostitution with lines such as 'The charming man is seized and captured', and 'A man says, to keep being beautiful you need money'. Most of Morrissey's Japanese fans, or at least those who were bilingual, boycotted the book and even the exceptionally well-mannered Kanako declared, 'The only salvation of this book is that the cover photo of a gladiolus expresses the world of Morrissey's lyrics.'

On 7 September 1991 Morrissey appeared at the Logan Campbell Centre in Auckland, New Zealand, the first date on what should have been a ten-day tour of Australasia. Security was slacker than it had been in Japan, and even when he was almost dragged head-first off the stage into the audience, few people grew too concerned. In a backstage interview with Jill Graham of the *New Zealand Herald* – specifically requested for her honesty, and the fact that she was also a fan – Morrissey lamented those journalists who, during interviews, had treated him like friends, only to stab him in the back by 'spicing up' their articles with disparaging remarks before submitting them to their editors. 'The only good pop-writer now is someone creased with cynicism who despises everything,' he said ruefully. 'I've been scarred too often. Nowadays I only speak to people who like me and who understand me. I feel I don't have to curtsy to anyone.' Jill Graham also asked him why there was so little dialogue with the audience between songs, though the response should have been obvious – 'I don't need to . . . there is an instant warmth and love which sometimes is overpowering.'

In Wellington, Morrissey was in fine form, but in Brisbane three days later he appeared on stage looking gaunt and unwell. A doctor was summoned after the show, by which time he had developed a temperature of 102°F, and viral flu was diagnosed, aggravated by acute sinusitis. There was no question of the tour being allowed to continue, and he returned to England at once, leaving his disappointed Australian fans with a brief slot in a chat-show, performing 'King Leer'.

On 29 September, hale and hearty once more, Morrissey played the Dublin Point, the first of seven British dates prior to his departure for America and the rounding off of the *Kill Uncle* tour. Though he was singing better than ever in his solo career, the British music press had sunk to an all-time low in that they now condemned practically every move he made. Adverse criticism of an artiste's work by a knowledgeable expert is one thing, but to pass spiteful, vitriolic remarks about their persona is unpardonable. Barbara Ellen's *Melody Maker* review of Morrissey's Hanley show was so vile that it is a wonder the singer did not consider taking legal action. There was, however, worse to come when an absolutely disgraceful recording appeared on the market. 'Morrissey Rides a Cockhorse', by an American group named Warlock Preachers, was released in a cover depicting the singer, whilst on the actual label was a pornographic cartoon with an equally filthy caption. Morrissey, not wishing to draw extraneous attention to such people, ignored them all.

Morrissey's concert at the Hammersmith Odeon was filmed by Fuji of Japan for transmission on their WOWOW satellite channel, and never released commercially anywhere else, which is almost a crime considering its quality as compared with the technically inferior *'Live in Dallas'* video. Fortunately, bootleg copies of the film did survive, and it is a veritable treasure for fans and 'outsiders' alike. After the botched translations of the lyric-book, Fuji commissioned the playwright Yuji Sakamoto to supply subtitles for the film, but these, according to Kanako, were 'coarse and inaccurate'. The work also had to be edited owing to an unpleasant incident with security after Morrissey had directed the first few lines of 'Driving Your Girlfriend Home' to a fan standing next to the stage. Heeding the invitation, the young man attempted to climb on to the platform, only to be grabbed by four bouncers and half-carried, half-dragged up the gangway. Morrissey observed what had happened, and promptly gave orders to his band to stop playing. He then asked the audience to excuse him whilst he sorted out 'this ugly sham of security', leaving the stage for almost fifteen minutes to become embroiled in a heated argument within the wings, but emerging victorious to resume his recital and transform the stage into an open house wherein all and sundry were welcome to get up and hug him.

The final leg of Morrissey's 17-date North American tour began in Vancouver on 28 October, supported by The Planet Rockers, a rockabilly outfit from Nashville. Most of the shows had sold out weeks in advance, despite a distinct lack of advertising and hardly any press interviews at all. At the San Francisco Shoreline Amphitheatre on Halloween many fans turned up wearing fancy dress, and Morrissey was particularly amused to observe a delegation of Teenage Mutant Ninja Turtles!

Morrissey's concert at the Pauley Pavilion, on the UCLA campus at Westwood, Los Angeles, was the first such event there since The Pretenders had taken it by storm in 1981, though sadly it was only to be memorable because of the horrors which took place. Word of the singer's 'difference of opinion' with security at the Hammersmith Odeon had winged its way across the Atlantic, and the atmosphere of the last few evenings had been more relaxed than usual. The Westwood authorities, however, stunned by the speed of ticket sales – 11,500 moving in just sixteen minutes – gave an edict that everyone should remain seated throughout the performance, leaving the sizeable pit embarrassingly empty. For an artiste like Morrissey, whose on-stage survival was virtually dependent on personal contact, this was tantamount to damming his lifeblood. During 'The Loop', his fourth song, he threw his tambourine into the audience, hoping to coax them into moving forwards. This did not work and after the song he announced, 'We're fully grown adults. If you want to stay in your seats, that's OK with me – but you don't have to!'

Morrissey may have anticipated the sudden rush into the pit, but he was unaware that the first few rows of seats were

loose, folding chairs. During the excitement of 'Sister, I'm a
Poet', the 'invasion' song from Wolverhampton, pandemonium erupted, for the upturned chairs acted as caltrops,
entangling hundreds of pairs of feet and sending fans career-
ing in all directions. Though some of the more sensible fans
helped security staff to rescue the injured, the lunatic fringe
were only interested in using the ones on the floor as bridges
to get to Morrissey, who called out before his next song,
albeit in vain, 'Please don't tread on anybody's toes!' His
'phenomenal strength', referred to by Linder Sterling, was
evident during the following song when a fan tried to grab
Morrissey, only to trip over the microphone wire and, cling-
ing to his thigh, find himself being dragged from one end of
the stage to the other!

Clearly, the concert could not be allowed to continue and
half-way through his ninth song, 'We Hate it When our
Friends Become Successful', two huge security officers
escorted him off the stage for his own safety. The band followed suit. There was the possibility of the concert being
resumed, and some fans did help to clear away the debris.
Morrissey, obviously distressed, spent part of this interim
period in the first-aid room talking to the injured, though of
the 50 or so casualties none was badly hurt. His return to
the stage, however, was considered too much of a risk, and
when the announcement went out that the building would
have to be vacated, some fans began smashing up seats and
setting off fire-alarms. One merchandising stall was over-
turned and looted. Several thousand dollars were allegedly
stolen from a till. By this time a television crew had turned
up to film the proceedings, and police in riot-gear were seen
beating fans, willy-nilly, with batons. Though entirely
blameless for the disturbance, Morrissey did offer to pay for
the damage. 'He looked so very, very sad – but he behaved
like the perfect English gentleman right to the very end,' one
reporter said.

A warning was issued prior to the concert at the San Diego

Starlight Bowl that anyone leaving their seat, for any reason, would be ejected from the stadium and not allowed to return. Only a hundred people were allowed into the pit – these had won tickets in a local radio competition – and this lack of ambiance seemed to frustrate Morrissey, who several times between songs 'played drums' by banging the microphone against his head.

In Santa Monica on 4 November, not only was trouble anticipated – it was actually *hoped* for by a television newsteam who turned up expecting to film 'the riot'. The concert had been announced by KROQ one weekday evening at 11 p.m., and the ticket office had opened just one hour later with restrictions of two tickets per person to discourage touts. This had resulted in the odd scuffle, though nothing serious, and the later report that 25 fans had been badly injured during the concert were exaggerated. According to Morrissey's personal assistant, Jo Slee, 'They were just a bunch of sweaty teenagers who happened to faint!'

From a personal stance, the Santa Monica concert was perhaps the most important event in Morrissey's current calendar, for amongst the guests were two former New York Dolls – the bassist Arthur Kane, and the guitarist Sylvain Sylvain had requested a meeting before the show, but Morrissey had been too nervous and the rendezvous took place afterwards in his dressing room where he must have been flattered to learn that they considered his version of 'Trash' better than theirs.

On 7 November, Morrissey sang in Minneapolis. The city had recently suffered sub-zero blizzards and was still under three feet of snow. It was almost as cold in Chicago the next day where the venue had been changed at the last minute. Many of the tickets for the UIC Pavilion had been bought by touts and resold for several times their market value, and being forced to exchange these for general-admission tickets for the Aragon Ballroom – necessitating a long wait before the show to ensure good seats or standing pitch – created

much ill-feeling amongst a small group of fans, who astonishingly blamed Morrissey for ripping them off. These
people would cause him untold distress sooner than they or
he knew it.

Before going on stage at the Nassau Coliseum, Long
Island, on 11 November, Morrissey granted an interview
with New York's WDRE radio, and though he seemed well,
he was very tired – the dramatic temperature changes
brought about by alternating between indoor and outdoor
arenas, the ravages of a harsh American winter and the
extensive travelling and personal appearances between
venues had taken their toll. Most of the questions centred
around the songs on the *Kill Uncle* album. Morrissey
insisted that he did not feel homesick, and that he was enjoying the tour enormously. He was obviously referring to the
mindless violence of the Pauley pavilion when he said, 'It
only becomes alarming when security *assumes* that it's violence and not passion. It's *always* passion, and the people
who get on to the stage are very gentle people who unfortu-
nately get dragged off by their hair and in some cases get
beaten up. It's a shame. I don't imagine anyone would go
through all the trouble of scrambling past the security to get
to the stage if they didn't mean it.'

After the concert, Morrissey was driven to his hotel room
in a state of near-exhaustion, and shortly afterwards he collapsed. As in Australia, the remaining eleven dates on the
tour circuit had to be cancelled and the true nature of the
aforementioned small but influential clique of turncoat fans
was revealed shortly afterwards – in an American fanzine –
when a complaint was lodged which suggested that the
singer's ego had so interfered with his professional integrity
that, unable to fill large venues and unwilling to be relegated
to smaller ones, he had elected to abandon his tour. As well
as being erroneous, this comment, aimed at an emotive performer who had played no fewer than 68 highly charged
concerts in six months, mindless of personal discomfort and

an almost paranoid fear of flying, seems particularly spiteful. And especially so when the target was a man who had once told an American reporter, with utmost sincerity, 'It seems that people like me more here than in any other country in the world.'

9

Hills of the North Rejoice!

'I always maintain that I'm very rarely interviewed, but persistently cross-examined,' Morrissey told Dermott Hayes of *Rage* at the end of 1991. 'Most pop personalities are literally so plain and dull, that anyone who appears to have a vaguely working brain comes across as conniving. Therefore I'm drilled.'

Morrissey had agreed to the interview only after hearing the journalist hail him as one of the few performers worth talking about or talking to. As with his previous interview with Paul Morley, the opening question was rather silly and pointless – 'Why are you still here?' – but aptly dismissed with a humorous but caustic, 'I can't think of being a postman.' Morrissey also admitted, in anticipation of being asked why his last handful of singles had failed to match the success of their predecessors, that so long as he could continue making records which *he* liked, he did not particularly care whether they sold or not. Record companies, as he had expostulated so many times in the past, and airplay, decided upon chart success. Quality had little to do with what actually reached the hit-parade. He also stated that, though not a very 'sporty' person, he did own several bicycles which he did not use as often as he would have liked, adding coyly, 'I think you have to have at least one other person to indulge – which applies to many things in life.'

There was a new song, one of his first collaborations with his guitarist, Alain Whyte, 'We Hate it When our Friends Become Successful'. A formidable component of his American tour – though many of his admirers there are unlikely to have grasped its North of England connotations – it had been given a flamboyant British airing at the 30th Amnesty International, televised on 28 December 1991.

No one had been made more aware of the North-South divide over the past decade than Morrissey, and from a purely personal stance no British song has so significantly linked an author with his subject – the fact that a Northern upbringing does not necessarily equate with pigeon-fanciers, coalmines and ferrets. 'I've never worn a flat cap – and I don't smoke Senior Service!' Morrissey said firmly.

There was another reason for the song, which was released as a single in 1992. Although he did not put his Victorian home in the attractive suburb of Bowden on the market, he was compelled to leave for a while when pestering fans got the better of him – banging on doors at all hours, peering through windows so that the curtains had to be kept closed day and night, and on at least one occasion actually breaking in. He also had to suffer the indignities of being frowned upon by 'certain locals', resentful of his success. He told journalist Adrian Deevoy in an interview for *Q* magazine, 'There's the most vicious sense of competition in Manchester – so many jealous, vile creatures. That's what "We Hate it When our Friends Become Successful" is all about. In Manchester you're accepted so long as you're scrambling and on your knees. If you have any success, they hate your guts.'

The recording, backed with three numbers from Morrissey's concert at the Hammersmith Odeon, was the brainchild of Mick Ronson, without any doubt the greatest producer he had worked with thus far, and it took him to a high point in his career which some claim might never be surpassed. Ronson attributed his cordial working relationship with Morrissey to their arduous Northern upbringing, telling Tony Parsons, 'It affects the way you look at the world, the way you deal with people. It affects everything.'

Born in Hull in 1946, Ronson had been one of the pioneers of British glam-rock, playing in a local group, The Rats, before a momentous meeting in 1970 with David Bowie which had led to The Rats becoming The Spiders From Mars and a collaboration with five million-selling albums (*The Man Who Sold the World, Hunky Dory, Ziggy Stardust, Aladdin Sane* and *Pin Ups*). During a visit to Paris in summer 1992, Morrissey enthused, 'Mick was responsible for Bowie's best work, there's no doubt about that. He's a very underestimated talent who combined showmanship with great humility. Working with him on my new album has been the greatest privilege of my life.'

Ronson had also worked with Mott The Hoople, Bob Dylan, and Lou Reed – arranging the latter's 1973 shocker, 'Walk on the Wild Side'. Far more important from Morrissey's point of view, he had worked with former New York Doll David Johannsen, a fact which enabled the singer to place him on a pedestal with comparative ease. Sadly, the album would be Mick Ronson's swansong, for he had recently been diagnosed terminally ill with cancer.

The new album was given the title *Your Arsenal*, doubtless an intentional play on words. Linder Sterling's monochrome photographs for the sleeve were also thought-provoking. Snapped on stage at the Nassau Coliseum, the singer was seen sticking his tongue out at the audience, and brandishing his microphone somewhat suggestively at crotch-height. Morrissey's stomach 'scar', we were reminded, came courtesy of Davyhulme Hospital!

For some time, Morrissey had been saying that he was looking to do a 'physical' album, and the first song, 'You're Gonna Need Someone on Your Side', is a perfect example of this, enriched with massive, unfettered glam-rock guitars, cleverly interspersed with crowd noises, pipes, ticking clocks and snatches of radio/television dialogue. Such is the freshness of its lyrics that one would be excused for assuming Morrissey had recently emerged from a lengthy period of soul-searching solitude, which of course he had not – quite the reverse, for some of the songs had been worked on with Alain Whyte during his recent tour, at a time when he had been under tremendous pressure. As such, the line, 'Give yourself a break, before you break down' could quite easily have been Morrissey's warning to himself, in view of the way he had been working so hard, often to the very limit of his strength.

There was no lyric sheet with the album this time, primarily because Morrissey wanted the album to be listened to for its overall value, with equal emphasis on the music and the melodies as opposed to just the words, which many fans allegedly studied for days before actually playing the disc! When asked by a sympathetic French reporter why he had recorded this album so soon after *Kill Uncle*, he said, 'One must hurry! Life is short!' – retrospectively regarded by some as a subtle hint that he was still dubious about continuing his career. The humour was still there, though, when a British journalist asked him how one set about making a 'physical' record and he replied, 'Well, you begin by unbuttoning your shirt . . .'

Your Arsenal was Morrissey's symbolic lament for the decline, if not the actual passing, of the British culture he loved so very passionately, and no song represented his feelings better than 'Glamorous Glue'. When asked what, in his opinion, was dead in the England of today he replied, 'England itself. Everything is influenced by American culture – everybody under fifty speaks American, and that's sad. We once had a strong identity, and now it's gone completely. A primordial role of our most insular personality comes from our being an island. I don't want every country to be alike. Nobody in England wants the tunnel, yet they've still built it. It'll cave in, I'm certain of that!'

In this respect – horror of horrors! – Morrissey told Jean-Daniel Beauvallet that he was *almost* missing the former British Prime Minister, adding, 'I never liked Maggie Thatcher, but she was right about Europe. We *have* to keep our distance if we want to retain our identity. If she was still in charge, England would be more independent. John Major is a twit!' The 'conservative' line of the song, of course, was but a harking back to typical Northern obstinacy – the fact that there were still thousands of Northerners who would vote for the Labour Party, regardless of whom they were electing, simply because of family tradition.

Morrissey said of 'We'll Let You Know', his parochial hymn to football hooliganism, 'I understand the level of patriotism, frustration and jubilation – the aggression, and why it must be released. When I see reports on the television about hooliganism in Sweden or Denmark, I'm actually amused – so long as people do not die.' When asked if he actually sympathized with these thugs he joked, 'Well, they have such great taste in footwear!' It is a sad fact, of course, that inasmuch as the bike-pedalling French 'Johnny Onion' or the Beer-Swilling Belgian are regarded by prejudiced anglophiles as the norm, so the archetypal Briton as seen through the eyes of jaundiced Europeans is the football hooligan. The song, however, enriched with turnstile noises and stadium screams, was greatly misinterpreted by the media – for the narrators are the hooligans themselves who, as 'the last truly British people you will ever know' and who 'descend on anyone unable to defend' offer the lame excuse that it is the turnstiles that make them hostile.

The most controversial song on the album, and unintentionally so, was 'The National Front Disco', a tremendous piece in a class of its own, which not unexpectedly brought the severest criticism from the blinkered section of the media which had haunted Morrissey for the best part of a decade. He explained to Adrian Devoy of *Q*, 'Whether you choose to write about wheelchair-bound people or the subject of racism, the context of the song is often overlooked. People look at the title and shudder and say whatever is in that song shouldn't exist because the subject, to millions of people, is so awful. I don't want to sound horrible or pessimistic, but I

don't think black people and white people will ever get on.'
The observation was to all intents and purposes an honest
one, and the song was inspired by the recruitment techniques
of the National Front – applicable perhaps more to the previous decade than the current one – which had involved their
distributing leaflets outside schools, much as Morrissey himself had championed animal rights during the film for
'Interesting Drug'. He climbs not into the skin of the oppres-
sor, but into that of the disillusioned parent, whose only
course of action is to lament, 'Where is our boy? We've lost
our boy!', whilst the otherwise well-raised youth opines,
'England for the English!' The objective of the song – the
lampooning of the National Front by associating its
allegedly tough-as-nails members with a disco, thus reducing
their ideals by suggesting they listen to the kind of music so
often dismissed by Morrissey as 'discofied nonsense' – was
very much clouded by the media's 'racist' tags, proving yet
again the singer's theory that a good many of his attackers
were still failing to 'dig beneath the surface' of his lyrics. He
told Robert Chalmers of the *Observer Magazine*, 'The phenomenon of the National Front interests me, like it interests
everyone – just as all manner of sexuality interests everyone.
But that doesn't mean that you necessarily want to take
part.' Even so, from a few quarters this smear campaign
would continue for some time. Indeed, it would soon
become worse.

The next three songs on the album – 'Certain People I
Know', 'We Hate it When our Friends Become Successful'
and 'You're the One for Me, Fatty' – were released as singles
in Britain and the closing number, 'Tomorrow', was released
in America. Lyrically, one of the most fascinating songs and
certainly the most moving is 'Seasick, Yet Still Docked'.
Morrissey said, 'You can sit in your room for months on end
and see nobody, and cry quite bitterly into your pillow
because the phone never rings – then you think of those
recent weeks, and of your situation, and you burst out

laughing at the absolute absurdity of life and expectation.'
The song, a long one, contained several stanzas inadvertently
linking it with the work of the legendary Belgian singer-
songwriter, Jacques Brel. Whereas Brel's gritty dialogue for
'Amsterdam', translated by Mort Shuman and covered by
David Bowie, reads, 'He so wants to belch, but he's too full
to try!' Morrissey politely declares, 'Tonight, I've consumed
much more than I can hold', and the overall theme of the
song with its ticking clock – time slipping away, slowly but
surely – is very reminiscent of Brel's 'Les Vieux', with the
despondency of unrequited love transferred from the elderly
couple to the sad young man.

Morrissey reminded one interviewer, quite casually and
with no hint of solemnity, 'All of us are working against the
clock in our own way. I tend to have a cheese butty and sit
back and relax. Everything eventuates. The day will arrive
when you and I are not on this earth . . . people who have a
sense of time and therefore urgency are quite fascinating!
I've been accused of paying too much attention to death, but
what's wrong with that? It's a pretty serious matter, especially when you're lying under the wheels of a double-decker
bus!'

Morrissey's ability, not always polemic, to surprise applies
to the penultimate song on the album, for after the hopelessness of 'We'll Let You Know' we are reminded that, for
those of us who have faith, the precognitive dream holds
good.

Gradually building up in a crescendo, Morrissey's voice
soaring to take on an entirely new strength and emotion, 'I
Know It's Gonna Happen Someday' possesses an optimism
which was put to the test several weeks before the release of
Your Arsenal by the appearance in summer 1992 of the
unofficial study of The Smiths which hit the music press –
and Morrissey – like a tidal wave.

Morrissey & Marr: The Severed Alliance, subtitled *The
Definitive Story of The Smiths*, was the result of three years'

investigative research – more than a hundred interviews, including an in-depth one with Johnny Marr which, according to Morrissey, the guitarist told him he had 'regretted enormously' – by Johnny Rogan, whose published work includes biographies of The Byrds, Neil Young, The Kinks and Wham!. Rogan's publicity agent claimed at the time that the author possessed neither fridge, television nor credit card and that 'on one occasion he wrote in isolation for an entire year without speaking to another human being'. It was also stated that Rogan changed his address every ten weeks, which might have been worrying for Morrissey's lawyers in the event of litigation. What really upset him was Rogan's statement to the press that he had spoken to Morrissey and that this was 'the true and unsanitized story of The Smiths'. The singer hit out in the most virulent fashion, issuing the first in a trilogy of *fatwahs* or death-wishes which afforded Rogan a tremendous amount of probably unexpected publicity: 'Personally, I hope Johnny Rogan ends his days very soon in an M3 pile-up!' When Rogan replied that this was fine because he did not drive, Morrissey announced, 'I hope he dies in a hotel fire!' Although he told Adrian Deevoy of *Q* that he had only squinted at a friend's copy of the book from across the room, before being driven to the index 'just to see who'd blabbed', he *had* read it, and he had been shocked.

It's promoted as the definitive story of The Smiths. Of course, the only definitive story is *my* story, if ever that's told. Johnny Rogan has interviewed anybody who bears a grudge against me. Any of the people who've been close to me over the past decade he has not got near . . . basically, it's 75 per cent blatant lies. The rest is reasonably factual. I made a statement when the book was published which said, 'Anybody who buys this book wants their head tested.' According to sales figures, a lot of people need their heads tested. A lot of people have bought it, a lot of people will believe it.

The Severed Alliance received mixed reviews from the press, and sold better than it might have done because of Morrissey's attacks on the author. Tony Parsons, writing for the *Sunday Telegraph*, called it 'a beautiful monster' and 'hugely entertaining'. Richard Smith of *Gay Times* on the other hand found much of it long-winded, if not boring. He wrote, 'After having waded through the book's first half, you feel ready to sit O Levels in modern Irish history and the Stretford secondary system.' Others criticized the book for its lack of a decent editor, and Rogan's tendency to juxtapose some events in Morrissey's personal life with the pop head-lines of the day. Thus we are reminded, not very politely per-haps, that the singer entered the world at a time when Elvis Presley was topping the charts with 'A Fool Such As I', and that the fantasy writer J. R. Tolkien was leaving the world as Morrissey was entering his fourth year at St Mary's – not exactly an earth-shattering revelation. Rogan later said that though he had not been perturbed by the 'death sentence' imposed by his subject, he had been 'hurt' by the '75 per cent blatant lies' tag. Morrissey, on the other hand, must have been extremely distressed when, a few months later, Rogan claimed that his work had earned him letters of encourage-ment from Andy Rourke, Mike Joyce, Craig Gannon, Stephen Street – and the singer's own father.

One year later, under the threat of a second kiss-and-tell Rogan volume, the hatred was still obviously there. 'If God exists, then Johnny Rat should be eaten alive by his alsa-tians,' Morrissey told Jean-Daniel Beauvallet. 'I'm serious about that. Rogan's underhand enquiries prove him to be a dangerous person who writes only lies. I could speak to him about this, but why should I? I'm not afraid of confronting anyone, but not just any imbecile. I insist upon at least a *minimum* of intelligence!' Rogan hit out at this statement sarcastically on 8 July 1993 in a last-minute radio interview aimed at promoting the paperback edition of his book by saying that Morrissey's attack had been 'a Freudian slip' and adding, 'I don't have German Shepherd dogs, but Johnny Marr does . . .'

Coinciding with the Rogan book were numerous announcements in the music press that Morrissey would be participating in the Glastonbury Festival during the weekend of 26–28 June 1992. A large number of tickets were sold and yet, only days before the event, a further press statement claimed that Morrissey had had an altercation with a member of his band and therefore decided to pull out. Needless to say, such a move caused a great deal of ill-feeling amongst the more impressionable of his fans, who were encouraged to believe that their idol had let them down . . . more so, that he did not even care about them. The true fans, of course, were only too aware that he would never have done such a thing, and few were surprised when it later emerged that he had not agreed to the event in the first place.

Patriotism was very much in evidence on 4 July when Morrissey appeared on the bill of Les Eurockéenes, one of the biggest and brightest events in the French music calendar which took place at Belfort. The ambiance was electrifying, particularly as the starting time of his concert (following Ned's Atomic Dustbin!) was twice delayed. Fearing a riot, the promoters sent out for several vanloads of flowers, and these were distributed to the crowd in the hope of placating them – a ploy which worked.

Morrissey took to the platform shortly before midnight. During his first song, 'Glamorous Glue', he wrapped a huge Union Jack around him. During 'November Spawned a Monster', he played, somewhat tremulously, the introduction on a violin (borrowed, it was said, from the rock-chanteuse Catherine Lara). There was also a cover version of 'My Insatiable one', a song by a then little-known group named Suede. This contained the lines 'On the escalator/ You shit paracetamol as the ridiculous world goes by' which were frowned upon by many French fans for not being in keeping with his 'gentlemanly' image. Neither was it considered appropriate for fans to applaud and yell, American style, during the songs themselves . . . even during highly spirited recitals by Johnny Halliday, Barbara, Véronique Sanson and Jean Guidoni, there has to be some decorum so that others may be allowed to listen to their all-important words. These artistes all performed at Les Eurockéenes, and Morrissey remarked, 'At times I would love nothing more than to sit on the edge of the stage and sing to a respectful silence, with the applause coming only at the end of my songs. Then the other side of me tells me that if that happened, I would probably feel like I had failed.'

Morrissey was asked why he had decided to follow in the footsteps of The Who, and several other groups, by wrapping himself in the Union Jack. 'These groups were archetypally British,' he replied. 'My impression is that we're all descended from the same family tree. Nowadays, there are too many English groups who only ever dream of becoming Americanized.'

A few days after Belfort, Morrissey appeared at the Festival de Leysin, in Switzerland, where not even the miserable weather and an on-stage fall robbed the evening of its magic. The show was relayed across Europe by Radio Suisse-Romande.

If foreign journalists were by and large only interested in reporting Morrissey's artistry, patriotism and wit, his overseas interview for the British press was all but dominated by the now obligatory chestnuts of sex and drugs – the latter drawing a confession from him that he had experimented with Ecstasy not once, but twice. He admitted, 'The first time I took it was the most astonishing moment of my life. I looked in the mirror and saw somebody very, very attractive. Of course, this was the delusion of the drug, and it wears off.' He added that he had been quite alone at the time, and that the experience had left him uninterested in drugs, concluding, 'I'm not prudish. I don't mind if other people take them, but it's not for me.'

Morrissey's interview with Adrian Deevoy was conducted at the Hôtel Bristol, no doubt a deliberate choice with its obvious *Carry On* implications, and the proceedings terminated within the red-light district of Pigalle-Blanche, where the singer told the photographer Hugo Dixon to snap him in what was for him a highly irregular but nevertheless amusing setting – framed against a backdrop of suggestive neon signs, and gazing indolently at the goods on offer in a sex-shop window! The interview itself, however, was probably not the light-hearted affair anticipated by the journalist. An amusing moment occurred when his slightly inebriated companion rushed up to the singer, gave his eyebrows a hefty tug, and asked if they were real. Morrissey responded with a, 'No, they're held on with Velcro!' Several questions actually angered him, particularly the one asking his opinion of 'The Morrissey Consumer Monkey', a vicious lampoon by the alternative comedian Vic Reeves. 'It was meant to be hurtful,' he said, once he had calmed down. 'Vic Reeves is a person who cannot close his mouth for three seconds because he feels he'll disintegrate into bowl of dust. He's completely loathsome.'

Meanwhile, in England a new single was released which took no time at all getting into the charts and establishing itself as one of that summer's most popular, hummable anthems. Taken from the *Your Arsenal* album, 'You're the One for Me, Fatty' is a catchy, up-tempo number with strains of Buddy Holly, though the setting is dreary Battersea with its 'hope and despair'. Once again, Morrissey champions the 'underdog', this time climbing into the skin of the comedienne Victoria Wood (the inspiration behind his lyrics for 'Rusholme Ruffians'), who whilst delivering a proclamation of love for her heavyweight magician husband, Geoffrey Durham, issues the portentous message, 'Promise you'll say if ever I'm in your way'. The song was backed with the misspelt ditty, 'Pashernate Love', titularly evoking the *Carry On* star Bernard Bresslaw's 1958 novelty hit, 'Mad Passionate

Love', and containing the plum line, 'Pashernate love could make your sister erupt into wild blisters and boils'. The CD/12-inch was augmented by 'There Speaks a True Friend', Morrissey's lovely, lachrymose ode to a departed confidante.

On 26 July, the day before *Your Arsenal* was released in Britain, Morrissey embarked on a brief non-singing tour of the United States, promoting the album by in-store signings, radio appearances, and by generally just being there. The visit paved the way too for his forthcoming tour of the country, with mass hysteria almost equalling his last concert run. A 'leaked-to-the-media' midnight appearance in a Michigan record store was particularly memorable. President Bush was in Grand Rapids but most of the attention was diverted to the quiffed British singer's arrival at The Vinyl Solution, where he was greeted by 2,000 screaming fans. Adding to the excitement was a surprise tie-in party hosted by a rock-club across the way. A few evenings later, Morrissey participated in a radio phone-in with Tom Calderone of Long Island's WDRE-FM. He was subjected to a barrage of mostly ridiculous questions. When a woman named Nancy called in with 'As a psychiatrist, I just want to know why you left the lyrics out of this album,' Morrissey responded glibly, 'Well, as a *psychiatrist*, why do *you* think I did?' Conveniently put in her place, Nancy hung up. The tour ended on 5 August when Morrissey was joined by his musicians, especially flown out from Britain, as guests on New York's *Hangin' Live With MTV* singing 'Certain People I Know' and 'You're the One for Me, Fatty'.

Your Arsenal was universally acclaimed as Morrissey's finest album since *Viva Hate*, and equal to if not better than anything he had ever done with The Smiths, the lamenting for whom seemed to be resurrected each time he brought out a record. It shot to number 4 in the album charts, and has since sold several million copies worldwide. One critic whose musical *raison d'être* had so obviously ended during that fateful summer of 1987 called it 'a kind of "Kenneth

Williams-meets-Laurence Olivier-down-on-the-rainy-pier-
for-pie-and-mash" that captured our hearts way back when'.
David Sinclair of *The Times* loved it, praising also the musicians for 'welding the motor of Morrissey's erratic inspiration to a golden chassis'. And whereas the general music
press were more interested in making personal remarks
about the singer than offering an honest critique of his work,
Select published a lengthy feature headed 'The Feast of
Steven', in which the album was in turn reviewed and vilified
by '15 top pop celebrities' who, with the exception of a mere
handful, did not know what they were talking about.
Morrissey's friend Linder Sterling – whose photograph did
not appear next to her quote, whereas Johnny Rogan was
depicted as a smashed-up car! – did know, and in a statement enthused, '*Your Arsenal* has Morrissey riding bareback
on rich, feisty guitars, glistening as he rises with the
audacity to still believe in the enduring embrace of the simple song . . . In quieter moments he dives deep into our ven-
tricles, wistfully celebrating his search for the domain of the
heart.'

The comedian Steve Punt said, 'He's at his best when using
understatement. "The National Front Disco", a very con-
ventionally structured song, sums up the pathetic xenopho-
bia that feeds fascism far more neatly than any more strident
right-on version could have done.' Brett Anderson, the singer
from Suede, speaking during the first week of August 1992,
could not have known that within a matter of days his own
words would ring true:

There are people who want to accuse Morrissey of
being racist. They'll add 'National Front Disco' to
'Bengali in Platforms', 'Asian Rut', 'Reggae is Vile',
'Hang the DJ' and so on. You can tell there's nothing
evil in what he sings. He's only mentioned the National
Front because it's part of the 70s, like putting a Vespa
on the sleeve of 'You're the One for Me, Fatty', or using

skinhead imagery. He's not a racist, but a regurgitator of what went on in his youth.

The last word may be left to Siobhan Fahey of Shakespear's Sister, who perceived well beyond the petty prejudices of her dubious peers to speak as a representative of those who really mattered – the fans.

He's my complete idol. I adore everything he does. He's completely unique, a totally brilliant lyricist . . . cosy and English . . . like a blanket you pull over you when you are feeling down. I love the way he can combine total macho rawness with overtones of glam and affectionately camp rockability. By their very nature, there aren't many pop icons around. You don't get many pop icons to the pound, not in this game.

10

Lodestar in Samite and Steel

The ska outfit Madness, famed for their rowdy anything-goes audiences, had originally planned Madstock – the event heralding their re-formation – to take place with a single concert in London's Finsbury Park on Saturday 8 August 1992. 30,000 tickets were printed, and by the time most of these had been sold the group were advised that with a big-name supporting act, the event had the makings of a celebratory weekend. Ian Dury, Flowered Up and The Farm were assigned to the bill, but the promoters suggested Morrissey, which delighted everyone. Morrissey told the French press, 'Madness are old friends of mine. I wouldn't have done it otherwise. Gallon Drunk will be there, and maybe The Kinks. Paul Weller *should* be there. The entire "British Family"! It will be an expressly British weekend – no rave, no rap, no Americans! Just Vespas, Union Jacks, and afternoon teas!'

Gallon Drunk, close friends of Morrissey's band, had in fact already been contracted to support him on his imminent American tour. They entered the proceedings, however, much to the chagrin of The Farm, who were so suddenly and dramatically dropped from the bill that they threatened to sue Madness and the promoters for loss of earnings.

Finsbury Park became Morrissey's particular Calvary, through no fault of his own. Earlier that day there had been a 'Troops Out of Northern Ireland' march through the streets of Islington, organized by the National Front who had paraded the Union Jack, adopted by the movement as its emblem, and regarded by a number of insensitive journalists

as a fascist badge as opposed to the banner of patriotism.
Thus, when sizeable pockets of this very extremist faction
were sighted, along with hundreds of skinheads, amongst the
Madness crowd, trouble was anticipated. The problem was
exacerbated by the hot afternoon, which had resulted in
many Madness fans getting drunk long before the show
commenced. These hurled abuse, and numerous projectiles,
at Morrissey and his band as they walked on to the stage,
their rowdy heckling quite easily drowning the approving
cheers of his fans. Many too were chanting for Madness, as
Morrissey's own fans had often chanted rudely for him during Phranc's support slot on the *Kill Uncle* tour. At Finsbury
Park, however, this rough element were clearly on the verge
of riot. During his second song, 'Glamorous Glue',
Morrissey draped the Union Jack about him as he had at
Belfort – the athlete Sally Gunnell had done so after winning
an Olympic gold medal, and during the finale of that most
British of events, The Last Night of the Proms the officiating
soprano had appeared in the guise of Britannia – but this
otherwise patriotic gesture, performed before the huge backdrop depicting two suedehead girls, proved too much for
that section of the crowd, a large one, that lacked the intelligence to differentiate between being British and nurturing
fascist tendencies. Matters only worsened during 'The
National Front Disco' when Morrissey was struck by a
water-bottle and forced to change microphones. Other thugs
threw coins – sharpened, which seems proof enough that this
gratuitous violence was premeditated. Finally, after a half-
hearted rendition of 'You're the One for Me, Fatty', and
looking very upset, Morrissey walked off the stage and his
musicians followed suit. Needless to say, he cancelled the
Sunday concert even when told that hundreds of fans were
already en route to the venue, and there was little likelihood
of their knowing what had happened. Soon afterwards, the
press office at EMI issued a formal statement, 'Morrissey is
extremely disappointed that Sunday's planned performance

could not go ahead due to the abysmal behaviour of a small group of loathsome yobbos. His management have requested the promoters to refund fans' money. A Christmas show is being scheduled for those who really want to enjoy Morrissey – without the aid of "stimulants".'

The Finsbury Park fiasco, of course, was welcomed as manna from heaven by the small section of music journalists who for some time had been sharpening their quills – not to mention their knives – in anticipation of the kill. Morrissey had already said to Jean-Daniel Beauvallet, 'Newspapers make up stories, hoping to bait me into calling them with *my* version of events. That's how low these people have sunk in order to get an interview. I prefer to leave them to it, hoping the readers will be able to work out the difference between truth and lies. Even so, I've been terribly, terribly hurt.' Beauvallet hit out most strongly against these critics during an interview for this book, saying, 'My several meetings with Morrissey, during and after The Smiths, were immensely rewarding experiences. I was forewarned by one British journalist who had once received the sharp end of his tongue that he was an extremely difficult taskmaster, that he was often contrary, but I can honestly say hand-over-heart that he is one of the politest, gentlest men I have ever met. The so-called *mauvaise réputation* which Morrissey has only in Britain is entirely the invention of the British music press. It would be so easy to run out of superlatives when discussing Morrissey. England should be proud of him.'

While several publications merely hovered on the brink of assassination, the *New Musical Express* grasped the proverbial bull by the horns and issued its own radio statement: 'Following more controversial lyrics on Morrissey's album, flirting as that song ['National Front Disco'] does with right-wing imagery . . . going on stage in front of a largely skinhead audience, waving a Union Jack – there are questions that need to be asked in the house, so to speak, and we've asked them. We are the People's Friend. He's flirting with danger.'

It was almost traditional that anyone appearing on the front cover of the *New Musical Express* had usually granted the paper an exclusive interview, and for the 22 August 1992 issue, the features editor had already decided upon a three-page spread on the Australian singer-actress Kylie Minogue. This was used, but the cover-photograph was replaced by one of Morrissey with the banner headline, 'MORRISSEY: FLYING THE FLAG OR FLIRTING WITH DISASTER?' What followed was a five-page résumé detailing every single 'culpability' predicted by Brett Anderson in his *Select* interview, and more besides. Proclaiming him 'a miserable, loveless outsider who flirts with racist imagery', it further accused him of neglecting fans by cancelling the end of his last American tour and by 'pulling out' of Glastonbury. It reproached him for his criticism of Johnny Rogan, and there was an entire page of 'Morrissey quotes' collected from interviews conducted by various publications over the last decade. Printed vastly out of context of their original interviews, many of these appeared harsher than they had been intended. Even more ridiculous was the column calculating how much the average Morrissey fan 'could have conceivably forked out this year not to see the Great Man *twice* . . . an astonishing £189.60 for nothing but disappointment.' An *NME* insider also revealed exclusively to me how the mammoth feature had been supervised by a 'Morrissey-friendly' journalist, without whose arbitration it could quite easily have developed into a lawsuit. Morrissey, when alerted to this diatribe by way of being asked to 'explain' himself, reacted as only he could by keeping his cool and issuing a brief, sensible statement, 'The *NME* have been trying to end my career for four years, and year after year they fail. This year they will also fail.'

The backlash was tremendous, though largely confined to the 'Angst' column of the *New Musical Express*, which over the next few weeks claimed to have received hundreds of letters, the authenticity of which, by reason of their poison-pen methods and vulgar pseudonyms, might excusably be doubted. Thus, Morrissey's defenders were seen to belong to the lunatic fringe and therefore to be eligible for ridicule by the editor, whilst his attackers were so vociferous that their outpourings might only be regarded as obscene and defamatory. There was even an 'open letter' feigning support for the singer from Johnny Rogan, who very soon added another string to his bow by collaborating with the Mancunian band, Family Foundation, on a track which must have angered Morrissey as much as if not more than *The Severed Alliance*. 'Red Hot' – basically an 'interview' between Rogan and Terry Christian (the presenter of Channel 4's *The Word*, who once claimed that he had known Morrissey at school) in which the alleged right-wing flirtation at Finsbury Park was debated most sarcastically – had been recorded in the 'ragga' style which the singer had never denied hating, and adding insult to injury was the presence of former part-time Smith, Craig Gannon. When asked what he thought Morrissey's reaction would be to the record, Rogan told *Select*, 'I don't care . . . he may well just ignore it. The best thing that could happen is that he'd give me a ring and talk it over.' Morrissey's response remains unprintable. Almost as bad was his treatment at the hands of a small group of individuals who founded a new British fanzine, flooding the publication with derisory remarks about Morrissey and virtually ignoring his music.

For some time, Morrissey allowed his accusers free rein over their prejudices, though in December 1992 he told Robert Chalmers of the *Observer Magazine*, 'I *like* the flag. I think it's very attractive. When does a Union Jack become racist? Now the press claim that every skinhead in London wants my blood, which is twaddle.' Several months later, when the controversy had died down somewhat, he was able to admit that the aftermath of Finsbury Park had not bothered him at all because he had not been guilty in the first place. And as per usual in these later years, he only really opened up to a non-British journalist, telling Emmanuel Tellier in an unabridged interview in *Les Inrockuptibles* in the summer of 1993:

> Not *all* skinheads are racists. Skinheads and the National Front are two *different* things. Skinheads are emblematic of the British working classes. I have no ties whatsoever with racism. I *do* like boxing – does that make me violent?

And on the subject of 'The National Front Disco' he seethed,

> The ones who listen to the *entire* song, the way I sing it and my vocal expression, know only too well that I'm no racist and glorifier of xenophobia. The phrase 'England for the English' is in *quotes*, so those who call the song racist are not *listening*. The song tells of the sadness and regret that I feel for anyone joining such a movement. And how can the English flag upset anyone? The Union Jack belongs to *everyone*, not just extremist parties. I AM NOT GUILTY . . .

Tony Parsons, writing for the *Daily Telegraph*, was one of the few British journalists to defend him.

> Personally, I don't think that Morrissey has a racist bone in him . . . I can't believe anyone who can write a song like 'Suffer Little Children' isn't on the side of the angels . . . My great fear is that Morrissey will become the Sarah Ferguson of pop, driven into exile by the cruel and uncaring media . . . Let us pray it doesn't happen. It would be a tragedy if the crown prince of pop suffered the same fate as the Sloane who fell from grace. Put down that flag, Morrissey. Your country needs you.

On 30 August, Morrissey entered London's Abbey Road

studios and recorded two songs – 'A Girl I Used to Know' and 'Jack the Ripper'. The latter expressed the narrator's desire to ensnare the man whose face is as mean as his life has been, 'If it's the last thing I ever do', which of course it would have been in a real-life situation. The reality, in fact, comes towards the end of the song when, in lush musical surroundings, Morrissey is able to link one aspect of his personality with that of the mysterious murderer. In France too the song was compared with *Lily Passion* (more of which later), an extraordinary musical play starring Barbara and the actor Gérard Depardieu which had opened at Le Zénith in January 1986.

A few days after this session, Morrissey flew to America for the first leg of his *Your Arsenal* tour, a gruelling 53-date schedule which would keep him occupied until the end of the year. Supporting him were Gallon Drunk, the rockabilly/electro-punk outfit fronted by James Johnston, who had just signed a contract with Sire, Morrissey's American label. Their biggest hit thus far, 'Some Fools Mess', had been nominated Single of the Month by the *New Musical Express* in November 1991.

The tour opened on 12 September at the Orpheum Theatre, Minneapolis, though this concert was memorable only in that it ended prematurely after a stage-invasion. This almost repeated itself three days later in Toronto, when 'The Girl Most Likely To' had to be transformed into a ten-minute guitar solo whilst Morrissey walked off the stage to confront security staff who had manhandled several fans into the wings and handed them over to the police, who charged them with civil disorder and arranged for them to spend the night in jail. Morrissey calmly signed the release forms, and the show was allowed to continue. A reporter from *Entertainment Weekly* who expressed surprise at Morrissey's angry off-stage outburst was told by him, 'I don't like it when people think of me as a wimpy, poetic, easily crushed softie. I'm quite the opposite. I'm a construction worker!' The *Toronto Star* thought along the same lines, saying, 'Morrissey sings like a choirboy – one who was abandoned at birth and raised by a family of bikers.'

This 'toughie' image was demonstrated throughout the tour by Morrissey's band. In Gainsville, Gary Day 'drowned' his guitar after 'The National Front Disco', and Spencer Cobrin trashed his drumkit with a microphone stand in New York – he and Alain Whyte were described by one journalist as 'like a couple of juvenile delinquents looking for their next purse to snatch'. The concert at New York's Limelight Club was delayed by several hours, and there was no support act. Tension was already running high when Morrissey shed his shirt to reveal the words SLIP IN written across his chest. Several songs later the proceedings were halted by the Fire Department because of overcrowding and this time Day smashed his guitar in a fit of pique.

Several shows attracted television news coverage, particularly the first of the two at the 13,000-seater Hollywood Bowl, which had sold out in just 22 minutes, eight minutes faster than one given by The Beatles. There were, however, greater problems than ever before with in-hall security. The San Antonio concert had begun with good intentions – when someone yelled out, 'Morrissey for President!' he quipped, '*Me* for President? Then you'll vote for Ross Perot?' – but soon afterwards he was forced to stop the show and issue a severe warning to several bouncers whom he had seen beating fans. He told Lorraine Ali of *Alternative Press*,

If I see somebody manhandled I become infuriated. I go slightly out of control – they treat them very aggressively and when I consider that I pay the wages of security, I don't think it's fair. Like at the Hollywood Bowl, you pay $45 per ticket, you're hammered into your seat, and you have to remain there. The only aggression that ever occurs at my concerts is purely from security.

In the same interview, Morrissey expressed some surprise over his phenomenal success in the United States – then promptly hit out at the alleged lack of support from the media.

> What I've achieved is completely pure. There's no hype involved . . . it's the kind of success that *Rolling Stone* magazine couldn't possibly be interested in. They'd rather interview Yoko Ono or talk to Julian Lennon . . . that's what makes American music quite sad, this enormous capacity *not* to recognize anything until it's gone. That's the history of the American rock press – they're never quite there. They were never there for Patti Smith, or for The New York Dolls.

This 'lack' of media coverage did not prevent Morrissey's US-only single, 'Tomorrow', from topping the University Charts. Housed in a sleeve depicting the swimsuit-clad singer lounging in Sunset Marquis with the latest copy of *Variety*, it told the only too familiar tale of the prevarication experienced during the quest for love – the fact that though the narrator, in this instance Morrissey himself, begs the object of his desires to put their arms around him and reassure him that he is loved, he cannot prevent himself from concluding, 'I know you don't mean it.'

The American tour ended at Philadelphia on 29 November, and the next day Morrissey and his entourage flew back to England. He had barely enough time to catch his breath – appearing on a number of television shows to promote his new single, 'Certain People I Know' – before embarking on a brief British and European tour. This was complemented by an excellent video compilation, 'The Malady Lingers On' (title courtesy of British comic Les Dawson), and 'Morrissey Shot', Linder Sterling's definitive photographic testimony of the *Kill Uncle* tour. And if many of the shots were posed, the ones which were not captured the singer's every mood – pensive, angry, cynical, smiling, sexual, despondent, even tearful. There was even an inadvertent study of what the French call 'Le miroir, la lampe et la rose' (the mirror symbolizing self-analysis, the lamp symbolizing the warmth emanating between the artist and his public, the rose for love), which deeply moved the editor of *Les Inrockuptibles*, Morrissey's favourite music publication. There was also a new manager in the bulky form of Nigel Thomas, a stalwart individual who had handled the affairs of ex-Kinks frontman Ray Davies and Sheffield-born rocker, Joe Cocker.

Ironically, a cold and wet Sheffield was the first date on the tour. Morrissey was supported by an excruciatingly noisy rockabilly outfit, The Well-Oiled Sisters, and for the author, witnessing his very first rock concert, the evening was something of an eye-opener . . . after a 45-minute interval spent in the smoky theatre bar, the lights dimmed without warning, and sheer pandemonium broke out as I fought to get back to my seat. In the wake of the *New Musical Express* accusations, there was not a 'suedehead' to be found amongst the piles of merchandise on sale in the foyer, and the backdrops had been similarly amended – Elvis Presley, a young and almost unrecognizable Diana Dors, and Charles Richardson, a gangland leader, rival of the Kray Twins, whose photograph had appeared on the inside of the *Your Arsenal* sleeve. The performance itself was nothing short of thrilling. I had expected him to be good, but what I heard and saw stretched way beyond my expectations.

Again, the press were unnecessarily severe. One well-known journalist, standing next to me at the bar, had turned to his companion and said, 'I don't care *how* good he is, he won't be getting a good review from *me*!' Another later criticized him for not speaking during his performance. Obviously this person knew little of the importance of continuity, the life-blood of those who communicate via their music.

At the Alexandra Palace on 19 December there were ticket concessions for fans who had missed out on Glastonbury and the second day of Finsbury Park, and there was a surprise guest-appearance by Kirsty MacColl, who sang The Smiths' 'You Just Haven't Earned it Yet Baby'. The next evening, at the Astoria, rumour spread like wildfire before the show that this would be Morrissey's last-ever concert in Britain, and it was both filmed and recorded for future video/audio release.

Two days later he played Le Zénith, in the Pantin district of Paris. For Morrissey and for myself, the wheel had turned full-circle. I had first become aware of his music in Paris some years before, and I had been personally involved in Le Zénith's opening back in January 1986. The venue had been especially constructed for Barbara – she and the actor Gérard Depardieu had starred in her musical drama, *Lily Passion*, a vehicle which would have suited Morrissey down to the ground. David (the name was an obvious choice) is a young serial-killer who, each time he hears Lily sing, goes out and murders someone. Eventually, Lily achieves her heartfelt ambition – like the hero of Morrissey's 'Jack the Ripper', to invite the killer into her arms, though in her case she is stabbed through the heart as they kiss after a last song. Since 1986 it has been traditional to record first nights at Le Zénith for album release, and Morrissey's 'first and last' was no exception. It was released on 10 May 1993 under the title, *Beethoven was Deaf*, and reached number 5 in the album charts. For reasons of copyright, parts of the performance were rearranged, and two songs were dropped and replaced by ones from the London Astoria master tape.

The period between the close of Morrissey's tour at Düsseldorf and the release of the new album was for him fraught with sadness. Elated that *Your Arsenal* had been nominated for a Grammy award (it was runner-up) he was devastated to be told of the death on 27 February of Tim Broad. The director of his best promotional videos was just

37, and had been ill for some time. 'Tim had extraordinary patience, kindness and benevolence,' Morrissey reflected. 'The cut-throat politics of the music industry never affected him.' Only a few weeks before, Morrissey's manager, Nigel Thomas, had suffered a fatal heart-attack, and at his Gloucestershire funeral he had praised the man who had done so much in so little time, saying, 'Ours is not a very dignified business, but Nigel managed to make it so.' Then, on 29 April Mick Ronson, the producer of *Your Arsenal*, died of liver cancer aged 46 . . . Morrissey's probably definitive album having served as his swansong.

No one may be sure exactly how deeply these tragedies affected Morrissey. He certainly became more reclusive than ever before, confessing that sometimes weeks would elapse without him so much as stepping outside his front door. Then, during the summer of 1993 came the shock announcement to Jean-Daniel Beauvallet of *Les Inrockuptibles* that his forthcoming album, *Vauxhall and I*, would be his penultimate . . . indeed, it could even be his last.

Several times during the recent past, the singer had expressed his dissatisfaction with the current music scene. There was too much rap, too much dance music, too little talent. Too many pop stars had passed their sell-by date . . . as in the world of popular song, the eagerness to walk on to a stage surpassed the ability to sustain the glories of what once had been. Morrissey himself had attacked some of these 'eternal teenagers' in his song 'Get off the Stage', and now he proclaimed that he had done, said and sung enough. The time had come to search for new horizons. He had already been approached for cameo roles in films – as a playboy in a film based on the life of Andy Warhol, and the part of Charles Richardson in a Krays-style London gangland drama. His pessimism, however, seemed to have reached an all-time low.

I want to do photography, to travel and to write . . . but

I've no desire to be recognized in the street any more. I don't really appreciate people. The ones that I care about are unreliable, and I no longer believe in human nature. The human race no longer interests me. I'm not concerned any more about the environment. People deserve to disappear. I'll be content when all the tigers, rhinos and elephants have become extinct – then they'll no longer be persecuted. Humanity deserves nothing more than to go up in smoke . . .

Epilogue
'Perlinpinpin'

During the summer of 1993, with the threat of his retirement hanging over his fans like the Sword of Damocles, Morrissey could have been found in a secluded studio, beavering away with fellow collaborators Alain Whyte and Boz Boorer. Of the fifteen or so songs actually completed, eleven would be selected for his new album, and others would be set aside to be used on the B-sides of his CD and 12-inch singles.

There was at least one cover-version of someone else's past hit. The Johnny Mercer-Henry Mancini classic, 'Moon River', had been sung by Audrey Hepburn in the film *Breakfast at Tiffany's*. Danny Williams had topped the charts with it in 1961, and both Gracie Fields and Henry Mancini himself had had hits with it. Morrissey's cover version owed much to his favourite Frank Sinatra version of the song. It was more than passable, though the CD extended version droned on for far too long, and he was criticized in some circles for changing the words to the standard – the line, 'It's waiting round the bend, my Huckleberry friend' was taken out.

Much more beautiful was a cover-version of a French song, George de la Rue's haunting 'Interlude' which had been composed in 1966 for the soundtrack of Carlo Ponti's film, *The 25th Hour*. Originally it had been included on the B-side of the Franco-Italian chanteuse Dalida's 'Hurt', and in 1971 it had appeared in English on Timi Yuro's *Something Bad on My Mind* album.

> Let's hold fast to the dream
> That tastes and sparkles like wine . . .

Who knows if it's real or if it's just
Something we're both dreaming of?
What seems like an interlude now,
Could be the beginning of love!

Morrissey recorded 'Interlude' as a duet with Siouxsie
Sioux, the singer with the seventies punk ensemble, The
Banshees, and it worked extraordinarily well . . . the blend-
ing of the gentle, effective baritone and the indigo tones of
the neo-torch singer make one lament that there have been
to date fewer exercises of the same quality. It was released in
Britain, after a Continental try-out, in August 1994.

For these new sessions, Gary Day and Spencer Cobrin
were gone, though they would turn up again for some of
Morrissey's television appearances, and may not have come
to the end of their particular road as far as touring with him
in the future may be concerned. His bassist for the new songs
was Johnny Bridgewood, the ex-Stingray who had played
bass-guitar on 'Sing Your Life'. The new drummer was
Woodie Taylor, formerly of The Johnson Family, who had
worked with Morrissey on two of his London dates during
the *Kill Uncle* tour. There was also a new, all-powerful
American manager, Arnold Stiefel, whose stable included
Rod Stewart.

The album – later hailed by the singer as 'The best record
I've ever made!' – was produced by Steve Lillywhite and
given the title *Vauxhall and I*. Music-press cynics quickly
pointed out that the area around Vauxhall Bridge was
Johnny Rogan's 'patch' – they had obviously forgotten their
earlier reports that he was in the habit of frequently changing his address. More famously, of course, the district was
the home of the Vauxhall Tavern, the legendary gay pub on
Kennington Lane, known for its good pint, its drag-queens,
and above all for its hospitality. Now that the building has
been added to 'Morrissey's London', the guide to the city
compiled by those fans who organize day-trips to those areas

mentioned in his songs or videos, one wonders what the patrons of the Vauxhall Tavern will have to say about the quiffed, inquisitive and largely uninitiated individuals who wander through its portals without knowing what to expect, and vice-versa.

'Hurrah, praise him, sing hosannas, the Mozzer is back!' is how one reviewer announced the release of Morrissey's first single from the album, which peaked at number 8 in the charts early in March 1994. 'The More You Ignore Me, The Closer I Get' was, for him, a rare love song in which the lover – Morrissey himself – is not only in full control of the situation, but is the one perpetrating the seduction by telling the would-be suitor that indifference will only make the situation more appealing. '*I've* made up your mind,' he declares, before warning, 'I bear more grudges than lonely High Court judges' just in case his quarry decides not to give in. The song was backed by the remarkable – even by Morrissey standards – love-pastiche 'I'd Love To', and the sublime lament for his unhappy childhood, 'Used to be a Sweet Boy', melodiously the most inspired song he had sung for some time, with lush, romantic orchestrations by Alain Whyte. One is almost a partner to the singer's burdening regret as he wistfully pronounces, 'Something went wrong and I know I can't be to blame'.

Vauxhall and I, released 14 March 1994, was applauded unanimously by the critics – indeed, it did not get one bad or even slightly adverse review – and within days it had topped the album charts. It is a gentler, more lyrically and spiritually rewarding album than any of its predecessors, a work of art par excellence. 'An inordinately beautiful record, certainly the most gorgeous Morrissey has ever done,' Andrew Harrison told me, and added in *Select*, 'If he keeps making records like this, you won't want The Smiths back.' 'This is magnificent,' enthused Caitlan Moran, in *Melody Maker*. 'Made in Gorgeous-O-Scope with supporting roles by Sarah Bernhardt and God.' The *Sunday Independent* declared it

'As homoerotic and darkly celebratory of things homosexual as anything the late Derek Jarman ever put on the screen.'

The eleven songs proved undoubtedly that, in a complex world surveyed through the poet's eyes, Morrissey's well of inspiration showed no signs of drying up. The opening song, 'Now My Heart is Full', centres around one of his greatest loves – the archetypal black-and-white British film. In this instance, the objects of his admiration are the thugs in Graham Green's *Brighton Rock*, the 'loafing oafs in all-night chemists' who are referred to by name: Dallow, Spicer, Pinkie and Cubitt. Amidst the vibrancy of engaging lyrics and a catchy tune, however, there lingers that undercurrent of angst and loneliness – the fact that, barring 'some rain-coated lovers' brothers', the narrator is still as basically friendless as ever.

The bouncy 'Spring-heeled Jim' has scattered in its lyrics snatches of Cockney dialogue from another film, this time the more recent *Let Him Have It!*, which tells the sad tale of the educationally subnormal teenager Derek Bentley, hanged in the early fifties. Again, there is considerable sexual ambiguity surrounding the alleged ageing member of the Richardson gang who will 'do' but never be 'done to', yet who has had 'so many women, his head should be spinning'. Here is the character who in his hey-day was afraid of no one, but now that he is past his best, bravado only begets regret as he laments, 'Where did all the time go?'.

In the film *Billy Budd*, based on Herman Melville's novel, the First Mate has a crush on the Beautiful Sailor (played by Morrissey's idol, Terence Stamp), only to betray him and see him hanged. There is also an opera on the story by Benjamin Britten. Scholars have recently asserted that this tale was founded on Melville's own unrequited love for the novelist Nathaniel Hawthorne. Morrissey's 'Billy Budd' draws an ingenious parallel not just between the demise of the Beautiful Sailor and his *own* wished-for demise by some sections of the music press, but in the prejudices experienced by gay couples who, thwarted by homophobes, are unable to find work.

'Hold on to your Friends' was described by Stuart Bailie of the *New Musical Express* as 'like Noël Coward with a harpsichord'. 'It was written about somebody I know, in relation to their treatment towards me,' Morrissey told William Shaw of the American magazine, *Details*. In it he speaks of the anonymous 'user' who only calls when he is in need of comfort and who at other times is impervious to his friend's feelings, reminding him that there are enough bad people in the world to criticize without attacking those he cares about. The song ends portentously, 'There just might come a time when you need some friends.'

The narrator of 'Why Don't You Find Out for Yourself?' on the other hand, makes a futile attempt to warn would-be artistes of the perils of allowing their mentors to manhandle their lives and careers in order to take advantage of the money they earn. It is a case of learning from the mistakes of one who knows – one who has truly found the glass hidden in the grass – although there is still scepticism from the other party, and Morrissey concludes with a shrug of the shoulders that he has been stabbed in the back so many times that he has no skin left.

In 'I am Hated for Loving', the singer allows himself to slip back into intense, crippling gloom – he becomes unwanted, unloved, attacked from all sides, not really belonging anywhere. He is simply 'falling, with no one to catch me'. Morbid irony, however, surfaces in 'Lifeguard Sleeping, Girl Drowning', which he performs in an unearthly, falsetto-type whisper. The song is a cross between Stevie Smith's 'Waving Not Drowning' and Byron's lament for Shelley, with a pleasing dash of Jacques Brel's 'La Fanette' thrown in for good measure.

This is the tale of the self-centred, attention-seeking woman – the 'nobody's nothing' who takes too much for granted, not least of all her indifferent, overworked lover

who, when she swims too far out to sea and gets into difficulties, casually allows her to drown. Her death is played in
the minor key whilst the elements are in the major.

'The Lazy Sunbathers', the only politically controversial
song on the album, epitomizes 'Les Enfants de Novembre' at
its most potent. Though written in the wake of the horrors
of Sarajevo, it harks back to the early days of World War II
when many Hollywood stars sailed for Europe, as part of the
Office of Strategic Services' courageous package which saw
them risking their lives entertaining our troops, whilst their
so-called peers saw fit to lie back and laze in the sun. 'They
thought the war was nothing to do with them,' Marlene
Dietrich told me. 'So they just lounged around all day, doing
nothing, whilst innocent people were getting butchered . . .'
In 'The Lazy Sunbathers' Morrissey reminds us of the cal-
lousness of these cold-blooded people.

Speedway is the name of the long, fashionable coastal
thoroughfare which runs through Santa Monica. During the
early fifties, with its wealth of uncloseted gay clubs, bars and
bath-houses, it formed part of the cruising area beloved by
rebellious actors such as James Dean, Montgomery Clift and
Rock Hudson. Today, it is one of Morrissey's preferred
sojourns and it may well be here, away from the sniping
British music press, that he feels completely at peace with
himself.

'Speedway', the symphony-in-miniature which closes
Vauxhall and I, begins colla voce and appears to be heading
towards the tenderness of 'There's a Place in Hell for Me and
My Friends' . . . until the ear-splitting revving-up of a chain-
saw directs it into an acerbic attack on Morrissey's oppres-
sors, those tabloid Shylocks out for their pound of flesh, who
attempt to break his spirit, but fail to do so quite simply
because there is nothing left to break. Even so, he is painfully
aware that he could be fighting a losing battle, as he declares
that his detractors will not rest until the hearse has claimed
him, silencing him forever.

On Tuesday 15 March 1994, the HMV record store in the middle of London's Oxford Street was witness to scenes of unprecedented hero-worship when Morrissey held his very first British signing session. The shop had estimated a crowd of around 500, as there had been for Tina Turner and Cliff Richard, and were pleasantly surprised when over 3,000 fans turned up from all over the country. There was even a contingent from Belgium who had camped out all night on the pavement. Morrissey turned up in the usual denims and Doc Marten boots, and wore a badge on the lapel of his tweed jacket reading FAMOUS WHEN DEAD. His famous quiff, observed Jim White of the *Guardian*, was 'like the dorsal fin of a killer whale in captivity'. Casually, he tossed a bunch of gladioli towards the long line of admirers – and missed. The flowers hit one of the press photographers, some say not just by chance.

The same scene, with the same-sized multitude, was repeated two days later at the HMV store in Manchester. On home territory Morrissey signed non-stop for four hours amidst scenes of sometimes uncontrollable emotion. One big, very butch-looking young man collapsed after kissing him on the cheek and had to be led aside and revived with a security guard's hip-flask. Bill McCoid reported in the *Manchester Evening News*,

> The fans are let through the barriers, the last steps towards their Holy Grail . . . He lets people hug him, he wrings their hands. It's not unlike the Pope giving an audience. This is as near to religion as you can get without the religion.

During the spring of 1994, two sharply contrasting interviews appeared in magazines in Britain and America. The ever-reliable Stuart Maconie, this time writing for *Q*, had met Morrissey not in some cloistered, claustrophobic location, but in a Battersea spit-and-sawdust pub on a busy

Friday night. The talk had been matey, and Northern. Though the magazine's cover declared 'MORRISSEY: "Yes, I am Pregnant!" – MR CHUCKLE-TROUSERS UNZIPS HIS LIP', and although the accompanying photographs had been snapped atop Hollywood's Griffith Observatory, where *Rebel Without a Cause* had been filmed, Maconie's actual interview was headed 'Goodbye, big-bloused flower-fondler; cheerio, depressed devotee of deathly doom; toodle-oo, tee-total football-fearing perma-hermit; we'll sithee, bespectacled Billy No-Mates!' This, of course, is what Morrissey was all about – like Gracie Fields, George Formby, Norman Evans and many more before him, his greatest quality was his no-nonsense Northernness. 'It never goes away,' he said proudly. 'That indelible working-classness.'

The topical subjects discussed by these two included the Gillian Taylforth alleged oral-sex episode – 'I don't think she did it, and I have nothing but sympathy for her.' The plight of British football, now that the disastrous England manager Graham Taylor was gone – 'I played football myself a few weeks ago and scored four goals, though I should add the game was against Brondesbury Park Ladies!' The recent incident when an assailant in Australia had fired blank shots at Prince Charles. Discussing royalty with Morrissey was like waving a red rag at a bull, and when Maconie asked him if he wished the bullets had been real, he could not help himself. Nodding, he replied, 'It would have really shaken British politics up . . . it would have made the world a more interesting place. One of them is bound to get it soon – could be me!'

On that other touchy subject, the British government, after declaring the country politically depressing he concluded, 'John Major is no one's idea of a Prime Minister, and is a terrible human mistake. If we focused on Clare Short or Harriet Harman, here are people with some personality. John Smith would be better suited to selling bread, and no one would buy it. It makes one long for Communism.' And of course, he still wanted to smack Vic Reeves in the face!

Much of Morrissey's acerbic wit seemed to be lacking from an interview featured in the American magazine *Ray Gun*, however, and towards the end of it he reverted to the pessimism which appeals to so many:

'I'm not sure what it is about life that's supposed to make it worthwhile . . . I've never really enjoyed life. I've never known how to.'

And on the subject of death: 'I'm not really frightened by death – it's not a particularly horrendous thing for me. I feel sad for other people, but not for me.'

'Not even if it's a complete full stop?' the interviewer asked. Morrissey smiled, 'That's fine by me!'

With half a dozen hugely successful solo albums and twelve years of at-the-top experience tucked under his belt, Morrissey was now the proven, undisputed hero of the contemporary British music scene. Yet some of those critics who had lauded *Vauxhall and I* were loath to grant him more than the customary five minutes of glory before launching into a wholly unnecessary, vitriolic attack on the responses he gave to two on-the-face-of-it pertinent questions. When Morrissey denounced the blandness of 'rap' music to an American journalist – the undeniable fact that all rap music *does* sound the same – he was accused once more of racism because rap is ostensibly a part of the black culture!

Equally ludicrous and exaggerated was the response to Morrissey's interview with Andrew Harrison, which featured in the May 1994 issue of *Select*. The interview and photo-session were conducted in and around the boxing-ring at the York Hall gymnasium in London's Bethnal Green, in the presence of Alain Whyte and Morrissey's companion-personal assistant, a closely cropped, burly young man named Jake who would later take a series of stunning pictures for Morrissey's record covers, and whose torso – emblazoned with tattoos and with the word MOZ across his midriff in large letters – had graced the sleeve of 'The More

You Ignore Me, The Closer I Get'. Morrissey is a great box-ing fan, and soon afterwards was seen on television, sitting at the ringside during the Benn-Eubank title-fight.

To a certain extent, the singer may have been courting crit-icism by appearing on the cover of *Select*, baring his teeth and wearing a knuckleduster, and he may also have been inadvertently sowing the seeds of discontent for the bigots and the 'unintelligentsia' when he confessed that though there had been a recent spate of television programmes about the National Front, he was baffled by the fact that the organization had never been given a clear voice or platform. When Harrison asked for his opinion as to whether this was a good thing—particularly if the National Front and the British National Party pursued their political goals through violence—Morrissey replied, "If they were afforded television time or unbiased space in newspapers, it would seem less of a threat and it would ease the situation. They are gagged so much that they take revenge in the most frightening way by hurting and killing people . . . part of that is simply their anger at being ignored in what is supposed to be a democra-tic society.'

In the usual tirade of complaints to the music press, all of them biased and some of doubtful origin, Morrissey was accused of 'sticking up for the democratic rights of racists', and many skeletons were dragged out of many cupboards. Few of these people realized that Morrissey was merely *expressing an opinion,* that he was examining the problem from another angle.

Long may he continue to do so!

Two important books were published in 1994. Jo Slee's excellent visual documentary, "Peepholism: Into The Art of Morrissey" was a trade paperback which housed illustrations of every Smiths sleeve commissioned by the singer, several more which were discarded, rare advertisements, articles, and a wealth of fascinating statements and anecdotes. "It opens Morrissey's mind and allows us to peer inside," declared

Travis Gravell, an affable young American who edits the equally fascinating "Wilde About Morrissey" fanzine.

Morrissey himself had spoken of these beautiful covers, on the eve of The Smiths' split, during a rare interview with the Flemish magazine, *Humo*.

> By using a photograph of Candy Darling or stills from long-forgotten films, you lay down a certain code: if you're a Smiths fan, together with us you think about certain films, actors, writers and photographers. It creates the soothing feeling that together we form one world. With The Smiths it wasn't *just* the records. It was mainly this added dimension ... there were so many people that *had* to be remembered and honoured on our sleeves.

"Landscapes Of The Mind" lost no time at all in reaching the best-sellers charts. It had been written expressly to please all the fans who had contributed to it, and succeeded in pleasing many more. They loved it, so did Morrissey. To me, this was all that mattered.

The sweat and sawdust of a provincial boxing stadium were foremost in Morrissey's thoughts during the summer of 1994 when he entered the Olympic Studios in South London to record five songs—the first single from this session, "Boxers", backed with "Have-A-Go Merchant" and "Whatever Happens, I Love You", was released in January 1995. Described by Pat Kane of the *Guardian* as, "One of the loveliest melodies and narratives Morrissey has yet penned, an aching tragedy of working-class hardness and celebrity," it only reached Number 25 in the charts, though at the time of its release thousands of Morrissey fans were counting the pennies, preparing their onslaught of the eighteen venues he had lined up for this "untitled" tour. This would be the most uncommercial tour of them all—few official posters, tee-shirts and programmes, and hardly any backstage passes.

The four kicked off on 3 March—a wet, miserable Friday—at the Glasgow Barrowlands. Supporting him were Joe Moss protegés Marion, a five-piece band from Macclesfield whom Morrissey had approved after seeing them in concert. From their first song onwards, the crowd yelled for Morrissey. Jaime Harding, the group's frontman, complained about this, though it would have been exactly the same no matter who was supporting. At *any* Morrissey show, the fans are only interested in seeing him.

As the lights dipped, gone were the raucous, blood-curdling tones of Klaus Nomi—replaced by the toneless but patriotic rendition of Blake's "Jerusalem" by the borstal boys from the soundtrack of "The Loneliness Of The Long Distance Runner." The backdrop was suitably more attractive than the last one—Cornelius Carr, the tousle-headed champion from the "Boxers" video also graced the back and front of the newly-released compilation album, "World of Morrissey". Gone too were the diaphanous and samite shirts, replaced by the more conservative 1960s Ben Sherman checks which, more often than not, stayed on throughout this tour. The denims were collector's items dating from 1944, and cost upwards of $2,000 a pair!

Morrissey opened with "Billy Budd", worked his way through most of the new album, a collection of recent songs, B-sides, with nothing at all pre-1991 ... dipping into the "archives" just the once to close with "Shoplifters Of The World Unite", the very last song The Smiths had sung live when they had appeared on *The Tube* in April 1987. This number was aborted halfway through, the next evening in Motherwell, owing to a quite aggressive stage invasion. Speaking of this somewhat unusual venue, Morrissey told David Sinclair of *The Times*, "I decided to play there because it's such a nice, round, comforting name." When asked by David Cavanagh of *Q why* he had chosen a Smiths song, he responded, "It's just as much mine as anyone else's. I wrote those words. It doesn't belong to some fictitious brickie from

Rochdale, it belongs to me." When Cavanagh complimented him on being one of the most superb speakers of the English language, he quaffed, "You're obviously confusing me with Syd Little!"

Craig McLean, covering the three Scottish concerts (the third was in Edinburgh) for *Spectrum* and *Vox*, was blinded with a fan's admiration and wrote, with utmost sincerity, "Like any god, Morrissey has his disciples. Like any disciples, Morrissey's feel compelled to record their own gospels and spread the word. The fanzine culture that has sprung up around the arch-Hulmerist is an international industry ... their mutual love of one man is why they're all standing in a carpark in Scotland in the middle of winter."

Fans entering Sheffield's City Hall on 7 February were handed a pamphlet informing them that the show was being filmed, adding in large letters: BY YOUR ATTENDANCE YOU ACCEPT THAT YOUR IMAGE AND OTHER RE-CORDINGS OF YOUR PHYSICAL LIKENESS & SOUND WILL BE CAPTURED AND USED IN SUBSEQUENT EX-PLOITATION OF THE CONCERT IN ALL MEDIUMS IN PERPETUITY. Morrissey was introduced by an overweight drag-queen, a Dockyard Doris lookalike who made the audience spell out his name. Because the event was being filmed, the front-line security actually encouraged fans to invade the stage and hug Morrissey ... and this show, like several others, ended up with him wearing a local vintage football team shirt.

Morrissey's concert in Blackpool was also filmed—the cameraman started off by capturing a skinhead fan entering the Empress Ballroom with a copy of "World Of Morrissey" tucked under his arm. Besides "Jerusalem", he was played onto the stage with a hefty section of Górecki's "Third Symphony", a work composed in tribute to those who had perished during the Ghetto Uprising in Warsaw during the German Occupation. This beautiful piece, which topped the

British album charts in 1993, also closed this and several other concerts.

Thenon, Morrissey played Cambridge, Birmingham, Bristol, Ilford Portsmouth, Hull and Bradford with seasoned verve. Despite having been recently "kissed" by the dreaded 'flu bug—"I'm afraid that I picked up something nasty in Hull!"—the singer was in sparkling form, without any doubt the most talented male singer I have seen in the last quarter-century. The next evening, in Newcastle, the security was unbelievably intense. Mark Nicholson, the editor of the Northern-based "Tatty Truth" fanzine, explained why.

> This was because of the damage caused by overzealous fans in the same theatre during the "Your Arsenal" tour. Moz sensed this repressed atmosphere, but continued singing. Then during "Shoplifters" he saw a fan being rather brutally restrained from mounting the stage. Stopping the song, he chastised the security man with a stern, "What on *earth* are you doing?" This got the biggest cheer of the evening. The song started again—there was a mass stage-invasion, Moz was knocked to the ground, and the concert ended immediately.

After Ipswich, Cardiff, Croydon and Brixton, the tour closed in spectacular fashion at London's Theatre Royal Drury Lane—in terms of location, timing, and sheer vocal dexterity one of the finest moments of Morrissey's career— witnessed by this author from the opulence of the royal box, no less!

At Drury Lane, Morrissey was more loquacious than ever. "You can either be as playful as you like, or you can be your own boring self!" he announced blithely, before executing a particularly wild and nifty "Spring Heeled Jim", and he was not to be disappointed. Taking advantage of the unexpectedly relaxed security, and urged on by a tuxedoed young fan named Darren *pretending* to be a security man, the stage was assailed by a maelstrom of admirers. A leggy, leonine young woman in a flouncy red dress hitched this up to her thighs, wrapped herself around Morrissey's middle, and "grabbed a handful" before being escorted off by bouncers. A handshake with another female in the front row went wrong and saw him dragged all but headfirst into the crowd. Emerging from this melée minus his shirt, he coyly remonstrated, "That was *very* enjoyable!"

After "The More You Ignore Me, The Closer I Get" there was more wit and a mighty roar of approval when Morrissey pronounced, seeming to weigh each word carefully as if wondering whether or not to add a few well-chosen epiphets, "You may have noticed that I didn't get a BTI Award last week . . . *and I was so relieved!*" He was referring to the BRIT Award for Best British Male Singer . . . presented to Paul Weller. The previous year, Morrissey *had* received a Q Award for Best Songwriter—not that he needed such over-hyped accolades to prove his work to the music business. Many of the artistes who have won these awards have, after all, proved to be little more than five-minute wonders.

Although a sudden flurry of over-excitement from a group of fans clambering onto the stage and virtually flattening him caused Morrissey to jump ship only seconds into his "Shop-lifters" finale, the true climax to the evening had already occurred after "National Front Disco", when before fading into a tender, tear-jerking "Moon River," Morrissey had stood stock-still throughout a full seven-minutes of multi-strobed, mind-blowing feedback—in the words of the *Evening Standard*'s Max Bell, "In silhouette like the noble savage,"—bathing majestically in the silver spotlight, as he had done all those years before when I had first seen him at the Paris Eldorado. This, however, was no mere "savage", arrogantly savouring the love of his clan. Thirty-six years on, Perdican was reborn.

Morrissey remains an enigma, though with the passing of

time he has become tougher, more cynical, and less tolerant
of that undistinguished but sadly powerful group of bigots
who by sheer misinterpretation continually attempt to
destroy his career. Any fan—and any detractor who is being
really truthful—would, of course, maintain that he is
indestructible! Such is his power, and his ability to give out
and accept love, that these people are more than willing to
forgive his every indiscretion. *Only* Morrissey could get
away with cancelling *two* eleventh-hour concerts at the prestigious Carnegie Hall for a reason other than sudden death!

Some critics, too, have stated over the last year or so that
his career may be on the wane simply because not all his
records get into the charts. The albums *always* do, but the
singles vary, a fault which lies squarely with the record company for trying to stretch what is taken from the albums far
too far. Morrissey's favourite period in pop-history, the sixties, never saw four or five singles extracted from the same
album. The record companies would not have done it, the
fans would not have been taken in by such apparent greed—
Morrissey himself has expostulated this time and time again.
He is beyond the stage where he has to rely on chart success
because he is no longer that kind of exclusively adolescent-
worshipped star. One may almost count on the fingers of one
hand the number of Top Ten hits achieved in recent years by
compatriots such as Tom Jones, Shirley Bassey or Engelbert
Humperdinck, yet these artistes only grow stronger and
more popular with each passing season.

"I can think of absolutely no pop performer who gets the
same response as me," Morrissey told Michael Bracewell, in
an interview for the *Sunday Observer* towards the end of his
tour. "I am never ignored. The sound is too Ortonesque and
the voice too absolutely real. I know that my music will last—
whether I die tomorrow or stop in five years time, it will be
remembered as something unique."

In this respect, and without wishing to compare him with
anyone (simply because he remains incomparable in his own

one-star sphere), one may hope that Morrissey's *true* career as an All Time Great has only just begun . . . so long as the ink continues to flow from that Wildean quill, so long as this is his wish. He may rest assured, however, that whatever he decides, his admirers will always be close at hand . . . even if only clustered around the gate of that crumbling cottage in Somerset.

Appendix I

The following represents Morrissey's complete recorded output as a solo performer from 1988 to the present day. Bootlegs are included and vary in quality as many have been issued more than once on different labels. Flexis and promos supplied to the trade or given away by fanzines and magazines are not included.

1988
'Suedehead'; 'I Know Very Well How I Got My Name' (HMV POP 1618 7-inch).

'Suedehead'; 'I Know Very Well How I Got My Name', 'Hairdresser on Fire' (HMV 12 POP 1618 12-inch); the CD POP 1618 also contains 'Oh Well, I'll Never Learn'.

'Everyday is Like Sunday', 'Sister, I'm A Poet' (HMV POP 1618 7-inch)

'Everyday is Like Sunday', 'Sister, I'm a Poet', 'Disappointed' (HMV POP 1619 12-inch) The CD POP 1619 also has 'Will Never Marry'.

Viva Hate: 'Alsatian Cousin', 'Little Man, What Now?', 'Everyday is Like Sunday', 'Bengali in Platforms', 'Angel, Angel, Down We Go Together', 'Late Night, Maudlin Street', 'Suedehead', 'Break Up the Family', 'The Ordinary Boys', 'I Don't Mind if You Forget Me', 'Dial a Cliché'; 'Margaret on the Guillotine' (HMV [CD] CSD 3787).

1989
'The Last of the Famous International Playboys', 'Lucky Lisp' (HMV POP P1620 7-inch).

'The Last of the Famous International Playboys', 'Lucky Lisp', 'Michael's Bones' (HMV 12 POP 1620/CD POP 1620).

'Interesting Drug', 'Such a Little Thing Makes Such a Big Difference' (HMV POP 1621 7-inch).

'Interesting Drug', 'Such a Little Thing Makes Such a Big Difference', 'Sweet and Tender Hooligan' (live) (HMV POP 1621/CD POP 1621).

'Ouija Board, Ouija Board', 'Yes, I am Blind' (HMV POP 1622 7-inch).

'Ouija Board, Ouija Board', 'Yes I am Blind', 'East West' (HMV 12 POP 1622/CD POP 1622).

1990
'November Spawned a Monster', 'He Knows I'd Love to See Him' (HMV POP 1623 7-inch).

'November Spawned a Monster', 'He Knows I'd Love to See Him', 'Girl Least Likely To' (HMV 12 POP 1623/CD POP 1623).

'Piccadilly Palare', 'Get Off the Stage' (HMV POP 1624 7-inch).

'Piccadilly Palare', 'Get Off the Stage', 'At Amber' (HMV 12 POP 1624/CD POP 1624).

Bona Drag: 'Piccadilly Palare', 'Interesting Drug', 'November Spawned a Monster', 'Will Never Marry', 'Such a Little Thing Makes Such a Big Difference', 'The Last of the Famous International Playboys', 'Ouija Board, Ouija Board', 'Hairdresser on Fire', 'Everyday is Like Sunday', 'He Knows I'd Love to See Him', 'Yes, I am Blind', 'Lucky Lisp', 'Suedehead', 'Disappointed' (HMV [CD] CSD 3788).

1991

'Our Frank', 'Journalists Who Lie' (HMV POP 1625 7-inch).

'Our Frank', 'Journalists Who Lie', 'Tony the Pony' (HMV 12 POP 1625/CD POP 1625).

'Sing your Life', 'That's Entertainment' (HMV POP 1626 7-inch).

'Sing your Life', 'That's Entertainment', 'The Loop' (HMV 12 POP 1626/CD POP 1626).

'Pregnant for the Last Time', 'Skin Storm' (HMV POP 1627 7-inch).

'Pregnant for the Last Time', 'Skin Storm', 'Cosmic Dancer'*, 'Disappointed'* (HMV 12 POP 1627/CD POP 1627) * Live in Utrecht.

'My Love Life', 'I've Changed my Plea to Guilty' (HMV POP 1628 7-inch).

'My Love Life', 'I've Changed my Plea to Guilty', 'Skin Storm' (CD, released in USA only).

'My Love Life', 'I've Changed my Plea to Guilty', 'There's a Place in Hell for Me and my Friends' (HMV 12 POP 1628/CD POP 1628).

Morrissey at KROQ: 'There's a Place in Hell for Me and my Friends', 'My Love Life', 'Sing your Life' (Sire CD 940184–2; USA release only).

'My Love Life', 'The Loop', 'Skin Storm', 'That's Entertainment', 'I've Changed my Plea to Guilty', 'Pregnant for the Last Time' (TOSHIBA CD TOCP-6906; Japan release only).

Kill Uncle: 'Our Frank', 'Asian Rut', 'Sing your Life', 'Mute Witness', 'King Leer', 'Found, Found, Found', 'Driving your Girlfriend Home', 'The Harsh Truth of the Camera Eye',

'(I'm) The End of the Family Line', 'There's a Place in Hell for Me and my Friends' (HMV [CD] CSD 3789).

1992
'We Hate It When our Friends Become Successful', 'Suedehead'* (HMV POP 1629 7-inch). * Live at Hammersmith Odeon.

'We Hate It When our Friends Become Successful', 'Suedehead'*, 'I've Changed My Plea to Guilty'*, 'Alsatian Cousin'* (HMV 12 POP/CD POP 1629, *Live at Hammersmith Odeon.

'You're the One for Me, Fatty', 'Pashernate Love', 'There Speaks a True Friend' (HMV 12 POP/CD POP 1630).

'Tomorrow', 'Let the Right One Slip In', 'There Speaks a True Friend', 'Pashernate Love' (CD USA release only).

'Certain People I Know', 'You've Had Her' (HMV POP 1631 7-inch).

'Certain People I Know', 'You've Had Her', 'Jack the Ripper' (HMV 12 POP/CD POP 1631).

Your Arsenal: 'You're Gonna Need Someone on your Side', 'Glamorous Glue', 'We'll Let Your Know', 'The National Front Disco', 'Certain People I Know', 'We Hate It When our Friends Become Successful', 'You're the One for Me, Fatty', 'Seasick, Yet Still Docked', 'I Know It's Gonna Happen Someday', 'Tomorrow' (HMV [CD] CSD 3790).

1993
Beethoven was Deaf: 'You're the One for Me, Fatty', 'Certain People I Know', 'The National Front Disco', 'November Spawned a Monster', 'Seasick, Yet Still Docked', 'The Loop', 'Sister, I'm a Poet', 'Jack the Ripper', 'Such a Little Thing Makes Such a Big Difference', 'I Know It's Gonna Happen Someday', 'We'll Let You Know', 'Suedehead', 'He Knows I'd Love to See Him', 'You're

Gonna Need Someone on your Side', 'Glamorous Glue', 'We Hate It When our Friends Become Successful'; live at Le Zénith, Porte de Pantin, Paris (HMV [CD] CSD 3791).

1994

'The More You Ignore Me, The Closer I Get', 'Used to be a Sweet Boy' (PARLOPHONE 6372).

'The More You Ignore Me, The Closer I Get', 'Used to be a Sweet Boy', 'I'd Love To' (PARLOPHONE 12-inch/CD CDR 6372).

'Hold on to Your Friends', 'Moon River' (PARLOPHONE 6383).

'Hold on to Your Friends', 'Moon River' [extended] (PARLOPHONE 12-inch/CD CDR 6383).

'Interlude'/'Interlude' [extended] (PARLOPHONE 6365).

'Interlude'/'Interlude' [extended]/'Interlude' [instrumental] (PARLOPHONE 12-inch/CD CDR 6365).

Vauxhall and I: 'Now My Heart is Full', 'Spring-heeled Jim', 'Billy Budd', 'Hold on to Your Friends', 'The More You Ignore Me, The Closer I Get', 'Why Don't You Find Out for Yourself?', 'I am Hated for Loving', 'Lifeguard Sleeping, Girl Drowning', 'Used to be a Sweet Boy', 'The Lazy Sunbathers', 'Speedway', (PARLOPHONE [CD] 7243 8 27797 2 8).

BOOTLEGS

Morrissey: Untitled. The first concert of Morrissey's solo career recorded 22/12/88, Wolverhampton: 'Stop Me if You've Heard This One Before', 'Disappointed', 'Interesting Drug', 'Suedehead' 'The Last of the Famous International Playboys', 'Sister, I'm a Poet', 'Death at One's Elbow', 'Sweet and Tender Hooligan'.

Posing in Paris. Recorded at the Élysée-Montmartre, Paris,

29/4/91 by Bernard Lemoin and broadcast on José Artur's *Pop-Club*: 'Interesting Drug', 'Mute Witness', 'The Last of the Famous International Playboys', 'November Spawned a Monster', 'Will Never Marry', 'Pregnant for the Last Time', 'That's Entertainment', 'I've Changed my Plea to Guilty', 'Everyday is Like Sunday', 'Piccadilly Palare', 'Suedehead', 'Trash', 'Cosmic Dancer', 'Disappointed'.

Higher Education. Recorded Utrecht, 1/5/91: 'Mute Witness', 'Will Never Marry', 'Pregnant for the Last Time', 'Everyday is Like Sunday', 'Cosmic Dancer', 'Disappointed', 'Our Frank', 'That's Entertainment', 'I've Changed my Plea to Guilty', 'Piccadilly Palare', 'Sing your Life', 'Asian Rut', 'King Leer', 'The Last of the Famous International Playboys', 'November Spawned a Monster'.

Morrissey London 1991. Recorded 20/7/91, Wembley Arena, this contains the entire performance: 'Interesting Drug', 'Last of the Famous International Playboys', 'Piccadilly Palare', 'Trash', 'Sing your Life', 'King Leer', 'Asian Rut', 'Pregnant for the Last Time', 'Mute Witness', 'Everyday is Like Sunday', 'November Spawned a Monster', 'Will Never Marry', 'There's a Place in Hell for Me and My Friends', 'That's Entertainment', 'Our Frank', 'Suedehead', 'Angel, Angel, Down We Go Together', 'Yes, I Am Blind', 'Disappointed'.

Nothing to Declare But My Jeans. Recorded 28/8/91, Osaka Castle Hall: 'Interesting Drug', 'Piccadilly Palare', 'Mute Witness', 'Last of the Famous International Playboys', 'King Leer', 'Sing your Life', 'Pregnant for the Last Time', 'November Spawned a Monster', 'Alsatian Cousin', 'Will Never Marry', 'Everyday is Like Sunday', 'Asian Rut', 'The Loop', 'Angel, Angel, Down We Go Together', 'I've Changed my Plea to Guilty', 'That's Entertainment', 'Suedehead', 'Our Frank', 'Disappointed'.

Morrissey in Tokyo. Recorded 2/9/91, Tokyo Budokan:

'Angel, Angel, Down We Go Together', 'Interesting Drug', 'Piccadilly Palare', 'Trash', 'Mute Witness', 'Last of the Famous International Playboys', 'Sister, I'm a Poet', 'Alsatian Cousin', 'Asian Rut', 'The Loop', 'King Leer', 'November Spawned a Monster', 'Everyday is Like Sunday', 'That's Entertainment', 'Cosmic Dancer', 'Suedehead', 'Our Frank', 'Sing your Life', 'Disappointed'.

Digital Excitation. Taken from the Japanese broadcast of the 4/10/91 Hammersmith Odeon concert: 'November Spawned a Monster', 'Pregnant for the Last Time', 'Alsatian Cousin', 'Interesting Drug', 'Mute Witness', 'My Love Life', 'Piccadilly Palare', 'Driving your Girlfriend Home', 'Everyday is Like Sunday', 'Sing your Life', 'The Loop', 'Suedehead', 'I've Changed my Plea to Guilty', 'Cosmic Dancer', 'King Leer', 'Disappointed', 'Our Frank', 'Angel, Angel, Down We Go Together', 'Asian Rut'.

Dreams I'll Never See. Recorded 9/7/92 at Leysin Rock Festival: 'Suedehead', 'Sister, I'm a Poet', 'The Loop', 'You're the One for Me, Fatty', 'Girl Least Likely To', 'Alsatian Cousin', 'Seasick, Yet Still Docked', 'Such a Little Thing Makes Such a Big Difference', 'My Insatiable One', 'Everyday is Like Sunday', 'Interesting Drug', 'The National Front Disco', 'November Spawned a Monster', 'Piccadilly Palare', 'We Hate it When Our Friends Become Successful', 'Disappointed'.

I'm a Poet. Part One, recorded 1/10/92, Colorado: 'Girl Least Likely To', 'November Spawned a Monster', 'Certain People I Know', 'Sister, I'm a Poet', 'Such a Little Thing Makes Such a Big Difference', 'Tomorrow', 'We'll Let You Know', 'Suedehead', 'He Knows I'd Love to See Him', 'You're the One for Me, Fatty', 'Seasick, Yet Still Docked', 'Alsatian Cousin', 'We Hate It When Our Friends Become Successful', 'Everyday is Like Sunday', 'The National Front Disco'. *Part Two*, recorded October 1992, Saturday Night Live: 'Glamorous Glue', 'Suedehead'.

Appendix II

The following represent some of the more interesting etchings from The Smiths' and Morrissey's rarities catalogue, though it is by no means exhaustive.

'Hand in Glove', 7in: *'Kiss My Shades'*.
'This Charming Man', 7in: *'Slap Me On The Patio'*.
'What Difference Does It Make?', 7in/12in: *'Sound Clinic'*.
'Heaven Knows I'm Miserable Now', 7in: *'Smiths Indeed/Ill Forever'*.
'How Soon is Now?', 7in: *'The Tatty Truth'*.
'That Joke isn't Funny Anymore', 12in: *'Our Souls, Our Souls, Our Souls'*.
'Bigmouth Strikes Again', 7in: *'Beware The Wrath To Come!/Talent Borrows, Genius Steals'*.
'Panic', 7in: *'I Dreamt About Stew Last Night'*.
'Ask', 7in/12in: *'Are You Loathsome Tonight?/Tomb It May Concern'*.
'I Started Something I Couldn't Finish', 7in/12in: ' *"Murder At The Wool Hall" (X), starring Sheridan Whiteside/You Are Believing, You Do Not Want To Sleep'*.
'Some Girls Are Bigger Than Others', 12in: *'Noh Girl Like Jaguar Rose'*.
'Viva Hate', *'Education In Reverse'*.
'Bona Drag', *'Aesthetics Versus Athletics'*.
'Kill Uncle', *'Nothing To Declare But My Jeans'*.
'Everyday is Like Sunday', 7in/12in: *'Nineteen-Eighty-Hate'*.
'Interesting Drug', 7in/12in: *'Escape From Valium/Escape to Valium'*.
'Interesting Drug', SPM 29: *'Motorcycle Au Pair Boy'*.
'Ouija Board, Ouija Board', 7in/12 in: *'Art, Any Road'*.
'Piccadilly Palare', 7in/12in: *'George Eliot Knew'*.

'Our Frank', 7in/12in: '*Free Reg, Free Ron/Drunker Quicker*'.
'We Hate It When Our Friends Become Successful', 12in: '*I Don't Know Anyone That's Happy, Do You?*'.

APPENDIX III

MORRISSEY FANZINES

GREAT BRITAIN:
A Chance To Shine: c/o Bruce Duff, 66c Loampit Hill, Lewisham, London SE13 7SX.

The Tatty Truth: c/o Mark Nicholson & Martin Hunt, 21 Moffat Close, Wibsey, Bradford BD6 3RL, West Yorkshire.

Art Any Road: c/o Emma Hall, Southmoor, Dry Lane, Christow, South Devon EX 6 7PF.

UNITES STATES:
Wilde About Morrissey: c/o Travis Gravell, 2429 Old Concord Road, Apt. 202c, Smyrna, Georgia 30082.

Glamorous Glue: c/o Joyce Louie, P.O. Box 190883, Brooklyn, New York 11219-0883.

True To You: c/o Julia Riley, 831 Beacon Street, 9100-266 Newton Centre, Massachusetts 02159

Morri'zine: c/o Nicole Garrison, P.O. Box 255733, Sacramento, California 95865-5733.

Sing Your Life: c/o Russ Seekatz & David Tseng, 3726 North Tucson Blvd., Tucson, Arizona 85716-1039.

The Darkened Underpass: c/o Sandy Lee, 2128 Via Estudillo, Palos Verdes Estates, California 90274.

CANADA:
The Loop: c/o Steve Bates, 684 Yonge Street, Box 72, Toronto M4Y 2A6, Ontario.

JAPAN:
Lucky Lisp: c/o Kanako Ishikawa, Kichise, 3-23-61, Suigen-cho, Toyota, Aichi 471.

EUROPE:
The Mighty Quiff: c/o Tristan, Brakelmeersstraat 4, 9830 St Marten's Latem, BELGIUM.

Speedway: c/o Fabio d'Antonio, P.O. Box 7, 64013 Corropoli (TE), ITALY.

Nothing To Declare: c/o Aubry Gillio, 135/28 rue Yves Decugus, 59650 Villeneuve d'Ascq, FRANCE.

Morrissey Drive Me Home: c/o Manuel Rios, Apdo 14298, 28080 Madrid, SPAIN.

Index